The Interim Pastor's Manual

Revised Edition

Alan G. Gripe

GENEVA

Geneva Press
Louisville, Kentucky

Scripture quotations from the New Revised Standard Version of the Bible are copyright © 1989 by the Division of Christian Education of the National Council of the Churches of Christ in the U.S.A. and are used by permission.

Grateful acknowledgment is made to the publishers and copyright holders for permission to reprint excerpts from the following:

In-Between Times, published by the Interim Ministry Network (IMN), 1996; Mead, *Changing Pastoral Leadership,* copyright © 1976 by the Alban Institute and Roy Oswald, *Power Analysis of a Congregation,* copyright © 1988 by the Alban Institute. Reprinted by permission of the Alban Institute, Inc., Suite 433 North, 4550 Montgomery Avenue, Bethesda, MD 20814-3341. All rights reserved.

Book and cover design by Jennifer K. Cox
Cover photograph courtesy of SuperStock
First edition

Published by Geneva Press
Louisville, Kentucky

This book is printed on acid-free paper that meets the American National Standards Institute Z39.48 standard. ∞

PRINTED IN THE UNITED STATES OF AMERICA

97 98 99 00 01 02 03 04 05 06 — 10 9 8 7 6 5 4 3 2 1

Library of Congress Cataloging-in-Publication Data

Gripe, Alan G.
    The interim pastor's manual / Alan G. Gripe — Rev. ed.
        p.   cm.
    Includes bibliographical references.
    ISBN 0-664-50002-1 (alk. paper)
      1. Interim clergy—Presbyterian Church—Handbooks, manuals, etc.
2. Presbyterian Church—Clergy—Handbooks, manuals, etc. 3. Presbyterian Church (U.S.A.)—Clergy—Handbooks, manuals, etc.
I. Title.
BX9195.G75   1997
253—dc20   96-43216

The Interim Pastor's Manual

Geneva Press, an imprint of the Presbyterian Publishing Corporation in collaboration with Union Theological Seminary in Virginia, is devoted to providing resources in the Reformed tradition dealing with the history, theology, and life of the Presbyterian Church (U.S.A.).

Contents

93917

Preface

Several changes in the life of the Presbyterian Church (U.S.A.) have called for this revised edition of *The Interim Pastor's Manual*. Among the more significant developments are changes in the *Book of Order* regarding the practice of interim ministry, continued growth in the number of churches employing interim pastors, an increasing number of pastors who are interested in this field of service, and continued development and refinement of the understanding of the art of interim leadership. The *Book of Order* provisions for interim co-pastors and interim associate pastors were added as the need to expand the possibilities for interim service became apparent to the church. Experience in several presbyteries led to another amendment to the *Book of Order* to prohibit an interim pastor from being called to be the next installed pastor, co-pastor, or associate pastor of a church where that person had served as interim pastor. In light of these changes, I have extensively revised, reorganized, and rewritten this edition to reflect the *Book of Order* amendments and current interim leadership practices in the Presbyterian Church (U.S.A.).

Since the publication of the earlier edition, I have myself become an interim pastor and have served five churches in this role, which also prompted numerous changes in the text. I have kept in touch with the national and local professional organizations of interim pastors, both Presbyterian and ecumenical. I continue to consult with individual interim pastors, with presbytery leaders, and with many of the leaders of interim training programs in presbyteries, synods, and General Assembly. All these relationships have provided the knowledge, energy, and enthusiasm that have made this revised edition possible. I would like to express particular gratitude to the interim pastors in the Genesee Valley Presbytery Interim Gathering whose thoughtful support and encouragement have nourished and guided me along the way for nearly five years.

Since the first publication more than ten years ago, the number of pastors serving in interim ministries has increased at least fivefold. Training programs have flourished; those at Ghost Ranch and Montreat have been filled to overflowing every year. The General Assembly's Office of Certification and Accreditation has worked with leaders of the Association of Presbyterian Interim Ministry Specialists and others to develop a program for certifying intentional interim pastors, which it administers from the headquarters in Louisville, Kentucky.

In spite of the increasing number of quality Presbyterian and ecumenical interim pastor training programs now available throughout the country, there is still a shortage of intentional trained interim pastors. There is an even more acute shortage of certified interim pastors. One result is that trained interim pastors are seldom unemployed. Another result is that churches often are forced to employ temporary pastors who lack an understanding of or training in interim ministry. This has led to some unfortunate experiences in a number of presbyteries, when temporary pastors have overlooked or misunderstood the dynamics and needs of the congregations they were serving. The information here attempts to remedy such problems, but the most effective response to the needs of the church today is for all interim pastors to complete the full sixty-hour training program offered by the General Assembly and by some synods and seminaries.

This manual was originally developed for the Joint Task Force on a More Effective Placement System of the Presbyterian Church in the United States and The United Presbyterian Church in the U.S.A. It was designed for four audiences: the interim pastor, the session, the congregation, and the presbytery committee on ministry. Others who are likely to find it useful are members of presbytery or synod staffs whose tasks relate to the leadership of congregations. Some sections deal with matters of greater concern to one of these audiences than to the others. It will be beneficial, however, for each group to understand all aspects of interim service.

Sessions exploring whether or not to seek an interim pastor will be interested in chapter 1, especially the sections that deal with choosing the right option and that list some advantages of interim ministry. Sessions seeking or negotiating with an interim pastor will want to give special attention to chapter 3, the section titled "How Does a Church Find an Interim Pastor?"; chapter 4, the sections on contracting and covenanting; Appendixes A, C, and D; and chapter 5. Persons who are considering becoming an interim pastor may want to begin by reading the first four chapters and chapter 11. Key members of the committee on ministry will want to be familiar with the entire manual.

A variety of special resources, ideas, examples, and models are included. Except for the quotations from the Presbyterian *Book of Order*, the entire manual is to be understood as advice and counsel, and each presbytery is free to establish its own policies and procedures. Relevant passages from the *Book of Order* are quoted or noted throughout the text. Every clerk of session and every interim pastor should keep a current copy at hand. Significant changes occur nearly every year. And congregations, sessions, and ministers should remember that specific guidance from presbytery will of course always supersede any advice offered in this manual.

It is desirable for each presbytery to approve formally a presbytery policy and procedure to guide the committee on ministry, sessions, and interim pastors. Many have already done so. It is hoped that this manual will be helpful in preparing such a policy statement.

Advocacy for the wide use of interim pastors and a desire to recruit more and better qualified persons to undertake this type of specialized ministry are additional reasons for preparing this manual. Presbyteries and synods themselves need to recognize why interim ministries are of critical importance to our church today. Further, governing bodies should have data available in concise and persuasive form to present to sessions the reasons for employing qualified interim pastors when they are needed.

Pastors themselves should understand both the opportunity and the challenge in serving as an intentional interim pastor. More qualified persons of all ages are needed who are willing to polish the special skills required for this particular ministry. Above all, recognition needs to be given to those pioneers in this field whose devotion to the church has inspired them to endure the difficulties that interim service sometimes imposes.

Many persons have shared in the development of this manual. Several doctoral dissertations, conference reports, occasional papers, and studies by pastors and church executives have served as background in its preparation. Numbers of church leaders, both laypersons and clergy, have read each draft and made many helpful suggestions.

I wish to thank all those whose participation made this manual possible. Mary V. Atkinson was especially helpful in the early stages of the development of interim ministry and the training programs that supported and refined the art, especially those at Ghost Ranch and Montreat, where I learned a great deal about the interim experience in the parish church. Donna Cook, the Associate for Certification and Accreditation for Interim Pastors, who continues to lead in the organization and development of these training programs, has been a real source of strength and encouragement. The faculty and students at these seminars, pastors, elders, church executives, and many of their spouses have made major contributions to this work. Their names make up a wonderful list far too long to be included here.

My sincere thanks to Anne Steele Young, whose superior gifts as a meticulous editor and whose understanding and experience as a pastor's wife assisted in numerous ways in correcting and editing this manual. To both my sons, Stephen and David, I express deep appreciation for their support and encouragement in all my ministry, but especially in the preparation of this manual. David has been nearby to strengthen me in most of my interim churches. Stephen's special knowledge and skills in computer technology saved me from many a near disaster with my own computer, and, just as important, he gave excellent advice and support in planning and editing the final draft.

Introduction:
There *Is* Joy

Rejoice in the Lord always; again I will say, Rejoice.
—*Philippians 4:4*

Ministers who have experienced the joy of working happily with the same congregation for a number of years, sharing times of rejoicing and times of sorrow, and who have then endured the grief of breaking the loving ties that develop in such relationships, find it difficult to comprehend that there can be real joy in relatively short-term interim service to a congregation. "Where is the joy?" they ask, as they consider the possibility of interim ministry.

A group of experienced interim pastors who gathered at Ghost Ranch were asked to reflect on where they found pleasure, satisfaction, and fulfillment in their interim work. They described personal joys, a genuine sense of freedom, excitement, and accomplishment, and professional joys, joys that come from skillful practice of a specialized vocation.

The personal joys these pastors experienced included the privilege of meeting new people, making new friendships, and helping others to grow in important ways. The interim pastor will always find satisfaction in the acceptance and inclusion that can develop quickly as the pastor models for the congregation the importance of actively making friends and promptly addressing both the individual and the corporate needs of the congregation. A sense of personal growth, which comes for the interim pastor as well as for the congregation, is often a result of these new relationships.

The privilege of travel to new and interesting places is another advantage many interim pastors have enjoyed, as they literally widened their horizons and deepened their appreciation of the world around them. Interim pastors, of course, are always more than tourists, since they actually live and serve for a time in these new places. Some who especially enjoy travel have found their interim ministry years among the best of their lives.

Even more important than these personal joys, however, is the satisfaction of the work itself. The interim pastor's creativity is challenged constantly by the discovery of how very different one congregation can be from another and by what special skills are needed in each call to service. Real strengths are clarified, tested, and polished, all in a setting in which the congregation is usually more open and patient because they know the interim pastor is new and unfamiliar with their church. Permission is more readily given to an interim to make some mistakes, especially in the first few weeks. This means the interim pastor can risk more innovation and careful experimenting than can an installed pastor.

Seeing a session grow in understanding its tasks, in taking ownership of its responsibilities as well as its privileges, in developing a vision of a new future for their part of Christ's kingdom—all this can be deeply satisfying. Such an experience gives both pastor and session energy and confidence, preparing them for a more vital and productive ministry. The whole congregation grows as the members, too, begin to undertake the special interim tasks that are theirs. The sense of achievement and anticipation they feel when they know they are truly ready to welcome a new installed pastor is gratifying to everyone, including the interim pastor.

One of the experienced interim pastor's greatest joys is to look back, after a year or two, at a church once served and find a strong installed pastor leading a vigorous congregation that has come to terms with its history, is clear about its own identity and mission, and is moving ahead into an exciting future.

Those interim pastors who shared their stories at Ghost Ranch concluded the conversation by recalling the joys of Jesus' own ministry, how he often spoke about the rejoicing there is when one lost sheep is found, one wandering son comes home to a loving father, one widow finds new hope for a future that seemed hopeless. They spoke about the satisfaction Jesus knew in feeding the hungry, giving rest to the weary, and bringing hope to the disconsolate. They likened Jesus' experiences in some ways to the sense of fulfillment they themselves had found in ministering to a discouraged congregation that attained a new vitality during the interim time.

Through the power and grace of Jesus Christ, interim pastors and the congregations they serve have the opportunity to find fulfillment during the interim time itself, not just in anticipation of a more satisfying future. For those interim pastors who had have this experience, there is real joy in knowing an important work has been well done in ministering to a church in a time of special need, the time that elapses between installed pastors. For those who have yet to enjoy the interim experience, I hope that this manual will inform, encourage, and inspire commitment to a rewarding specialized ministry—service as an interim pastor.

1

The Meaning of Interim: A Time and a Person

An interim pastor is one who temporarily assumes the leadership of a congregation that is without an installed pastor while a pastor nominating committee (PNC) is at work, or of a congregation where the presbytery's committee on ministry (COM) expects that a PNC will soon be elected. This manual is designed primarily for interim pastors. It also may be useful to those who are interested in understanding the tasks of the interim pastor, of the congregation, its members and officers, and of the presbytery and its leaders during the interim period.

The term *interim*, as used here, means a pastor who serves for a limited period of time between two permanent pastors while the congregation, through its elected PNC, is conducting its work. This interim person is called "pastor" or "minister" because the work covers most or all tasks of an installed pastor, as well as special tasks that are usually needed only during the interval between installed pastors. These special tasks include guiding the congregation's grief work over the loss of their previous pastor, preparing for a variety of changes in the ministry and mission of the congregation, and readying the congregation to accept a new installed pastor.

Successful completion of these assignments generally requires the experience, skill, and focus of intention that qualify interim ministry service to be considered a specialized form of ministry. Many congregations, on the advice of their presbytery or on their own initiative, are now calling interim pastors for a variety of special assignments. The majority serve as head of staff or as solo interim pastors; others serve as interim associate pastors or interim co-pastors. A search committee may take a few weeks longer to find a pastor when there is an interim pastor serving the

congregation. However, the result generally is a better match between the new permanent pastor and the church because the PNC
has not been pressured by the session or congregation to speed up
the search. Equally important, such congregations are usually better prepared to receive a new pastor after having had an interim
pastor, particularly if the interim pastor, the PNC, and the presbytery have all done the tasks that need to be completed during
the congregation's interim experience. This means longer, more
satisfying pastorates and therefore fewer pastoral changes because
of a dissatisfied pastor, congregation, or presbytery.

Other Interim Consultants

The term *interim* is also sometimes used to describe specialized
consultants who are called to serve a congregation or a governing
body for a limited time to perform a specific assignment. Some
possible examples of this situation are as follows: to conduct a survey of the congregation or community; to assist in goal-setting for
redevelopment; to solve a specific problem, such as a congregational or staff conflict, a budget crisis, or a program question; or
to meet some other specific need that present church leaders are
not equipped to handle. Interim specialists are also being employed today in executive positions in presbyteries and synods and
in the General Assembly offices. In addition, a variety of church-
related institutions, such as hospitals, schools, and colleges, make
use of interim professional personnel. A term that covers such
forms of interim service today is *interim ministry specialist*. Although this manual focuses primarily on the pastor who serves a
session and a congregation, other interim specialists will find the
information and guidance offered here to be worthwhile no matter what type of temporary assignment may engage them.

Steps in Changing
Pastoral Leadership

When a pastor leaves a congregation, or some other major staff
position becomes vacant, a sense of loss is often felt by the congregation, leading them to look longingly to the past and to grieve
for the person who has left. The redeeming quality of this moment, however, is that it also provides an excellent opportunity to

look forward. It is a time when a truly constructive ministry is possible, one that can have lasting benefits. It is an excellent time for renewal.

In his 1976 book *Changing Pastoral Leadership*, Loren Mead, founder of the Alban Institute (provides resources for congregations and religious organizations), listed seven steps involved in the process of finding a new pastor for a congregation:

1. The period of closure: the time after announcement of the decision to leave until the pastor's actual departure.
2. The period of direction-finding: the congregation (or session) learns how to proceed and what help is available.
3. The period of self-study: the congregation conducts a mission study to see what kind of leadership it needs.
4. The period of search: the congregation's representatives seek to find the pastor they want to call.
5. The period of negotiation and decision: the search narrows to one candidate, a decision is made, and an agreement is negotiated.
6. The period of installation: the new pastor arrives and is installed in office, officially and unofficially.
7. The period of startup: the new pastor and the congregation begin working together, and define each other's roles.

While Mead notes that this list may be misleading if too rigidly applied, it can serve as a useful frame of reference here for consideration of the interim pastor's tasks and of the work of the congregation, the presbytery, and others during the search processes.

As the seven steps are completed, it is important to note the various feelings that are usually experienced by the congregation: (1) relief or anger over the pastor's leaving, (2) guilt over some aspects of the past, (3) insecurity about the present and the future, (4) recognition of the reality of the situation, (5) awareness of the need for some help, (6) hope for the future, and (7) excitement about the new pastor. Understanding and responding supportively to such feelings are significant parts of the interim leader's task, a task that is complicated by the fact that these feelings may be experienced at different times and in different ways by various members of the congregation. Further, there is seldom a neat or steady progression from one step to the next, whether one considers groups or individuals. The goal is to bring everyone in the congregation (or as many as possible) to the final step, a joyful kind of excitement about the new pastor. The person who can lead a congregation safely through these various and conflicting kinds of feelings deserves to be called a specialist.

Varieties of Interim Leadership

Whenever a vacancy occurs, the presbytery COM extends its care to the congregation by counseling with the session concerning the kinds of temporary pastoral services available during the interim time. Before examining interim ministry in detail, other options provided in the *Book of Order* should be reviewed.

There are six categories in Presbyterian government under which ministers may temporarily serve a church that is without a regular pastor: "stated supply, interim pastor, interim co-pastor, interim associate pastor, temporary supply, organizing pastor" (*Book of Order* G-14.0513). It is unwise to assume automatically that choosing the interim category is best for most congregations while they are seeking a new pastor, though that is the most frequent choice. Indeed, some presbyteries require all congregations seeking a new pastor to employ an interim pastor while the search is under way. The COM may want to lead the session in a study of several of these categories before any decision is made. (In certain special situations the COM will suggest to the session or the congregation the calling of a designated pastor [G-14.0501g] rather than an interim pastor. Because the designated pastor is installed, that position is not regarded here as a temporary relationship and will be discussed later in this chapter.)

Choosing the Right Option

The presbytery's committee on ministry should study all the options carefully so that when needs arise it will be possible to determine accurately which category will be the best in each case. The following three options are most frequently used by churches seeking temporary leadership.

Stated Supply—Is normally approved in one of three circumstances: (1) when the congregation is not prepared to work through the customary search process, resulting in the expectation of a longer interim period; (2) when the congregation, the COM, and the presbytery committee responsible for mission planning all agree that full use of the usual search process would not be appropriate or helpful (for example, when there is no expectation that the congregation can call a new pastor or when on a long-term basis a congregation can only afford part-time staff who are not to be installed); and (3) when filling the pastoral vacancy involves arrangements with personnel or churches of other denominations (federated churches, for example).

Interim Pastor—Is normally approved when the expectation is that the congregation will move through the pastoral search process in the usual fashion, resulting in a call to a pastor, and when interim services are needed on a full-time or part-time basis for a period of six to twelve months at a time.

Temporary Supply—Is normally approved when the services to be rendered are limited in time or scope. This category will not be discussed here, since it is outside the concerns of this manual.

Some advantages in calling an interim pastor instead of a temporary supply are obvious. The session does not have to concern itself about who will be the preacher next Sunday. The major pastoral services that the congregation needs to sustain itself in a strong position are provided. Perhaps most important of all, the very title *interim* suggests that the congregation is between pastors, will be actively seeking another pastor, and will soon be ready to begin a new chapter in its life under a strong new leader.

The Interim Pastor

The *Book of Order* states:

An interim pastor is a minister invited by the session of a church without an installed pastor to preach the

Word, administer the Sacraments, and fulfill pastoral
duties for a specified period not to exceed twelve
months at a time, while the church is seeking a pastor.
. . . The session may not secure or dissolve a relationship with an interim pastor . . . without the concur-
rence of the presbytery through its committee on ministry. A minister may not be called to be the next
installed pastor, co-pastor, or associate pastor of a
church served as interim pastor or interim co-pastor
(G-14.0513b).

What are the major differences between an interim pastor
and a stated supply? The initiative in calling an interim pastor
is with the session; a stated supply is appointed by the presbytery
after consultation with the session, and initiative in the reap-
pointment of a stated supply generally comes from the COM.
The interim pastor serves a church during its search for an
installed pastor; the stated supply serves a church that is *not*
seeking an installed pastor. Both positions are not to exceed
twelve months at a time, and both may be renewed if all parties
to the agreement approve. In both cases, the COM has a
role and the presbytery must concur. An interim pastor may
be appointed moderator of the session, if all parties agree,
and need not be a member of that particular presbytery to
serve as session moderator, unless that presbytery, through its
COM or its stated clerk, decides otherwise. The stated supply
may serve as session moderator only if that person is a member
of the presbytery involved and the presbytery agrees. Further,
the *Book of Order* requires that before a stated supply is reap-
pointed for an extended assignment in the same church, the
COM must review that person's effectiveness. Even though
the *Book of Order* does not require a performance review for
an interim pastor, some COMs ask for it, and the wise interim pastor will seek an evaluation with the session or the session's personnel committee at midterm and at the close of the
interim.

It should be pointed out that the rule just quoted that pro-
hibits an interim pastor to be called as an installed pastor of a
church previously served also applies for interim associate pastors (G-14.0513c). The reasons for this will be discussed later.
The *Book of Order* is silent on whether or not a stated supply may

be called as the next installed pastor of a church that person has served as stated supply. Experience suggests that when the *Book of Order* is silent on a particular question, it is wise to consult with the presbytery's stated clerk as to what may or may not be allowed.

The Designated Pastor

The designated pastor is chosen for a short-term installed pastorate. As with the interim pastor or stated supply, one of the significant advantages in choosing a pastor for a temporary relationship is that the time without a pastor is greatly shortened. When a PNC is at work, it may take a year or longer to find the right pastor. When one of the temporary kinds of pastor or a designated pastor is the choice, the search for that person can often be completed in a few weeks. This is greatly to the advantage of a congregation that is suffering anxiety and confusion over the loss of a respected and beloved pastor. Most of the members will want a replacement as soon as possible.

In troubled times a congregation needs consistent pastoral leadership. That is one of the main reasons why the designated pastor position was created. While the *Book of Order* provides that "all the sections on calling and installing a pastor shall apply" (see G-14.0502–0507), that calling process can be greatly shortened by the COM when it provides a list of designated pastors for the PNC. *The New Committee on Ministry Handbook* suggests that a list of up to five names of ministers previously screened and interviewed by the COM be given to the PNC seeking a designated pastor.

The interim pastor provisions in the *Book of Order* do not specify how a congregation's interim pastor search committee will get names of candidates, but the COM should supply a list that helps cut down the search time.

How is the designated pastor different from the interim pastor? First, the designated pastor is installed and therefore is always the moderator of the session. Second, the designated pastor can be guaranteed a term longer than one year at a time; the provision in the *Book of Order* is for two to four years. Third, the designated pastor can become the "permanent" installed pastor after the designated term is completed, if all parties to the call agree. Because the designated pastor is installed, this minister has a different standing with the session, the congregation, and the presbytery. This category is listed here simply as one option the COM or the session may want to consider before deciding to ask for an interim pastor.

Circumstances When Interim Pastors Are Desirable

A number of special conditions can create the need for an interim pastor's services. Some of them are listed here:

1. The pastor or staff member has resigned, retired, or died, is on an extended disability leave, or is in some other way incapacitated, and the congregation needs guidance and support.
2. The congregation needs preparation for a new style of ministry, especially after a particularly long pastorate. (When this is the case, the next minister is likely to be an interim pastor, whether intentional or unintentional.)
3. The presbytery has removed a pastor and there is conflict within that congregation and hostility toward the presbytery or the COM.
4. There have been long-standing feuds or an unusual crisis in the congregation's life, and healing is needed.
5. The pulpit vacancy coincides with a sudden change in the character of the neighborhood or an unusual mission opportunity.
6. The church is declining or for other reasons needs the special expertise of supplementary staff.
7. The leaders of a congregation or presbytery want to expand the vision of a particular congregation.
8. There is an installed pastor, and that pastor and session wish to test an experimental ministry for a specific task and for a limited time.
9. There is an installed pastor, and there is a gap in the program of the church that needs attention but does not require additional permanent staff.
10. A continuity of pastoral and administrative leadership

and qualitative and quantitative improvements are desired during a pulpit vacancy.

Additional dimensions of interim service are suggested by consideration of the size of the congregation seeking temporary pastoral leadership. Many small pastorless churches are struggling to keep alive. They are a major care in nearly every presbytery, and yet little has been done in recent years to revive them. With the matching of the rich background of some retired pastors as part-time interims, spiritual and numerical growth and loving pastoral service can develop the potential in a given situation and prepare the congregation for an installed pastor.

Another option for such a congregation is the stated supply. Too often, however, the stated supply sees the task as purely maintenance, which may be what the small struggling church has already endured too long. A pastor trained in guiding planned change, someone with experience in a wide variety of positions, is more likely to meet the needs of a viable small congregation: in other words, a trained interim pastor.

When a sizeable church is without a pastor, there are several possibilities for interim service. One pastor could serve as the interim with the primary assignment of such sustaining tasks as worship, preaching, and pastoral care, thus offering stability to the congregation until the new pastor arrives; another could be called as a short-term consultant on a particular problem, such as conflict management. Churches with a multiple staff at times find it helpful to call two or three interims, one to serve as interim head of staff (IHOS) and the others as interim associate pastors (IAPs), each with clear job descriptions and accountabilities. In almost every kind of vacancy an interim can be helpful. Presbytery representatives should present clearly to the session of a church the benefits that such a pastor can bring. Some presbyteries feel so strongly that interim pastors are desirable that they require interims wherever a PNC is at work.

Advantages of Interim Ministry

A key advantage of the interim pastor's work is the objectivity and opportunity that come with its temporary character. The experienced interim is free to deal with a congregation's grief over the loss of the previous pastor. Concerns arising out of the previous pastorate can be worked through to help the congregation avoid projecting past difficulties onto the new pastor and enter the new relationship with fresh hope, vision, and confidence. It is often easier to make significant changes in the congregation because the interim pastor is free from a long-term personal investment. Also, the congregation may try out, on a low-risk basis, other leadership and new styles of ministry and worship.

Churches have also experienced other kinds of advantages in using an interim pastor. The PNC is more likely to be free to work carefully and without undue pressure from the congregation or the session. Worship attendance level is generally maintained and sometimes increased. Congregational life remains vital and gains direction because the interim can provide continuing leadership for existing programs and services and offer some creative innovations if desired. A good interim pastor often will serve as a specialist in such areas as stewardship, Christian education, or development of administrative manuals for use by the session. In addition, the interim, by listening carefully, can call attention to familiar and therefore tolerated abuses, such as needed building repairs, accepted interpersonal alienations, ineffective programs, and neglected areas of congregational life. Financial giving often stabilizes, and sometimes it increases. The interim gives the benefit of accumulated wisdom from previous situations and provides a fresh perspective on this church's life and mission. If he or she makes a special effort to build trust between the congregation and the presbytery, the presbytery can be experienced as genuinely positive, supportive, and caring. It can be a time to strengthen connectional ties by involving governing body staff and others as guest preachers in interpreting the broader church. Above all, the interim pastor's chief goals are to provide leadership during the pulpit vacancy and to prepare the congregation for the next installed pastor.

What an Interim Pastor Should Not Do

An interim pastor should not expect to do any of the following things:

Operate independently from the COM or the session.

Support one group in a power struggle over another.

Be expected to advise the PNC (unless requested to do so by the COM).

Promote any particular candidate for the pulpit.

Initiate major long-range programs or structural revisions in a congregation's organization (such initiatives belong to the session).

Consider being, or be considered as, a candidate for installed pastor.

The COM or the moderator should explain to the session and the congregation that the interim pastor is not to be considered as a candidate for the vacancy. It is wise for the interim pastor also to make this clear to the congregation when introduced and at other appropriate times. Experience indicates, however, that pressure may still be applied to the interim to consider such a call.

The interim pastor needs to understand why there may be many in the congregation who will want him or her to stay on permanently. This understanding will help the interim to be humble in spite of the congregation's acclaim. In the Interim Ministry Network newsletter *The In-Between Times*, the Reverend Clark Hargus, an interim pastor for the Disciples of Christ, wrote:

1.   The competent Interim Pastor is a model of effectiveness, and the people begin to see values in the Interim which they want continued. Good relationships are built and the interim congregation does not want to face the grief of breaking ties.

2.   There is less risk involved in keeping the Interim Pastor than in hiring someone unknown. Most churches have made mistakes in calling pastors, and they do not want to risk making another.

3.   It would be convenient and less expensive to keep the Interim Pastor.

4.   Interim ministry as a professional clergy choice is not understood by the laity. The professional Interim Pastor is relatively new in the church. Until the professional choice is understood, the people will think that the pastor in interim work is looking for something

permanent. Naturally they will think permanence is the preference and try to help by hiring the Interim.

Why does the *Book of Order* prohibit the installation of an interim pastor? The simplest answer is that experience in a wide range of presbyteries has proved the wisdom of this provision and the dangers inherent in allowing the interim to be a candidate for the installed position. The candidacy is sure to confuse the session and the congregation as to the pastor's own goals and purposes, it will confuse the issue as to the proper goals and purposes for the congregation in this period, and it will develop hidden agendas in so many people that rational, objective, and unencumbered decision making becomes nearly impossible. In addition to diverting the interim pastor and the session from the real goal of the interim period, which is to prepare the congregation for a new and different future and for the leadership of a new and different pastor (see chapters 5 and 6 of this manual), the congregation and perhaps even the session may become politicized and divided. Further, for the interim to become a candidate short-circuits the work of the PNC and often creates deep resentment.

Objectivity and Integrity

An interim pastor who openly or secretly desires to become the installed pastor has already lost the objectivity that is one of the position's major advantages, for he or she must be careful not to offend "important" persons or groups in the congregation. If education, discipline, mission development, conflict resolution, or other changes are needed, the interim who wants to be a candidate is not likely to jeopardize the chances of getting the call by risking direct confrontation. Prophetic but unpopular leadership or preaching may be needed but not provided. Such considerations do not face an installed pastor, for the installed pastor already has the call. The differences in the dynamics of the two situations are considerable.

In addition to objectivity, another key word in the interim pastor's relationship is integrity. The interim position was created as an intentional and specialized form of ministry and should be undertaken in that spirit. Experience indicates that churches thrive best when the expressed intentions and purposes of interim ministry are faithfully honored. Integrity is the cornerstone on which successful interim ministry is built.

2

Understanding
Interim Ministry

Interim pastors, or pastors who serve in similar functions to those described in this manual, have been part of Presbyterian church leadership since our earliest years. Today, however, it is apparent that a temporary pulpit supply is by no means the equal of an experienced, trained specialist in interim ministry. The development from one to the other has been a slow process. Interim ministry as a specialty has matured as the church has grown in numbers and diversity, as church programs and pastoral care services have become more complex and varied, and as governing body executives and officers in congregations have realized that every congregation has special needs when it lacks an installed pastor. Changes in the secular society around us and new appreciation of the dimensions of interpersonal relations and group dynamics have helped the church to think more carefully about the "in-between time" and the opportunities and dangers it presents.

Presbytery, synod, and General Assembly leaders, for the most part, now realize that any organized approach to a personnel service for church leaders needs to provide for appropriate, knowledgeable, temporary leadership while a search committee is at work. Recognition of the role of the interim pastor and the consequent need for a better understanding of that role have followed the recognition by the churches of their need for a better understanding of the installed pastor's role. One of the first organized efforts to study the role of the interim pastor was initiated by the Alban Institute early in the 1970s, and this agency has continued to lead in publishing high-quality resources. The Alban Institute was also responsible for calling together the first interim pastors' conference in 1975. Presbyterians were represented and supported all of these programs related to interim ministries and also began their own seminars and study programs at the General Assembly's national adult study centers, Ghost Ranch in Abiquiu, New Mexico, and Montreat Conference Center near Black Mountain, North Carolina. A variety of training programs, some introductory and some more in depth, have been offered by several synods and presbyteries.

The development of matching and placement services for interim ministries in Presbyterian churches has been a gradual process. In the 1950s, the Department of Ministerial Relations (then in Columbus, Ohio) and the Commission on the Minister and His Work (in Atlanta) both kept an informal roster of pastors, primarily retired, who were interested in interim service in parishes. These services have now been expanded and will be described later in this manual.

Most Protestant denominations with call systems, in which the congregation elects its own pastor, such as the Baptists, the United Church of Christ, the Disciples of Christ, and the Reformed Church, are now using some kind of interim pastor program to guide congregations through the search period. Even denominations with bishops who appoint pastors to congregations, the Episcopal Church and the Lutheran Church, for example, are finding that the use of interim pastors during the time between installed pastors is a healthy, gratifying experience for the congregation in transition. Many of these churches conduct their own interim pastor training programs, for which they publish their own resources. The prospects are good that the use of interims will continue to grow in all churches, whatever their system for finding new pastors. Even some Roman Catholics have inquired of Presbyterians and others as to the nature and practice of this program. The Interim Ministry Network, an association of professional interim pastors, has members from twenty-five denominations and continues to grow.

A Short Theology
of Interim Ministry

Understanding interim ministry means, first, understanding ministry and, second, understanding how ministry is modified when it is consciously undertaken at a specific place for a limited time and purpose. Every member of the church is a minister called to serve that faith which all believers, in whatever time and place, share in Jesus Christ our Lord. Edward Huenemann pointed out that this means a personal commitment, not to some private faith but to a universal, catholic faith. Further, this ministry is not only to a local congregation of Christians but to the apostolic church, a church sent and on the move throughout the world. The itineration of the early apostles in the then known world was visible evidence of the apostolic nature of the early church. Interim pastors today (because many of them are highly itinerant) share a special, privileged calling much like that of the apostles Peter and Paul, Silas and Barnabas. A real sense of commitment to a special mission is needed for an interim pastor to be willing to move almost every year.

These "marks" of the church, catholicity and apostolicity, are essential criteria for its ministry. All pastors, whether installed or interim, are called to serve the common universal faith (catholicity) and the outgoing mission-minded church (apostolicity). An interim pastor's ministry is specialized because it is more clearly defined as to duration and scope and because it is more focused on particular tasks to be begun and completed in a limited time.

The installation of a pastor is full of promise and danger. The promise rests in the opportunity the pastor's leadership can provide for the people's participation in the catholicity of the faith and the apostolicity of the church. The danger in every installation rests in the temptation of any congregation to assume that, because they have a pastor, this pastor is now obligated to serve the parochial interest of the congregation and not the catholic interest of the faith or the apostolic interest of the church. Quite imperceptibly, self-service can replace the apostolic calling in the nature of the church's ministry. For this very human reason, having an interim pastor (one who is like an apostolic visitor) in a local congregation, at the invitation of the session and the assignment of the presbytery, is significant. This transitional presence provides both continuity and symbol for ministry. The notion that installed pastors have ministry on a permanent basis is a dangerous illusion. An effective interim pastorate can be an excellent reminder that every congregation needs to be on the move, both in spiritual and in physical, material ways, reaching out into new experiences of life in the Spirit and new forms of mission and service to the world. Every congregation needs to become apostolic and risk being sent into the world to discover the universal truth (the catholicity) of the Christian faith. Without concrete change in a congregation's pastoral leadership from time to time, it could easily settle for less than the experience of the holy catholic and apostolic church.

Every ministry is limited by time and scope. What is distinctive about interim ministry is that termination is specified at the beginning. Further, sometimes there are specific tasks assigned by the presbytery or the session. If so, the assignment is usually more limited than that for an installed pastor. In some cases the interim is even specifically requested not to undertake certain pastoral tasks. All this is designed to accomplish carefully selected purposes during the time of transition in preparation for another leader.

Biblical Precedents

Biblical precedents come easily to mind. John the Baptist, who proclaimed "The one who is more powerful than I is coming after me" (Mark 1:7) and "Prepare the way of the Lord, make his paths straight" (Mark 1:3), had his own special tasks: to preach repentance and baptize those who believed. These acts were to prepare the people for a new day and new leadership. At the end of a relatively brief ministry, John pointed to one who was called by God to take up ministry among the people. His words about Jesus then were, "He must increase, but I must decrease" (John 3:30).

Jesus' ministry was distinctly interim and itinerant. He never established a home for himself. His active ministry covered only three years. As he traveled throughout the countryside and in the villages and cities, he was constantly preparing disciples to succeed him. "The one who believes in me will also do the works that I do and, in fact, will do greater works than these, because I am going to the Father" (John 14:12). Jesus spoke these words to all Christian believers, and they apply to installed pastors as well as interims.

Another perspective is suggested by the passage in which Paul writes, "I planted, Apollos watered, but God gave the growth" (1 Cor. 3:6). In other words, Paul saw his mission as a shared ministry, a continuation of the work performed by others earlier, to be taken up by different successors later on, in all of which the grace of God is at work. In many of his letters Paul delineates some of the very problems an interim frequently faces today—church conflict, for example. In 1 Corinthians 1:10, Paul wrote, "Now I appeal to you, brothers and sisters, by the name of our Lord Jesus Christ, that all of you be in agreement and that there be no divisions among you, but that you be united in the same mind and the same purpose."

The apostle also recognized that there are termination points in every ministry; it is recorded in Acts how Paul worked and preached for a limited time in many cities throughout Asia and then moved on (Acts 13:1–3; 14:1–3). Paul's farewell to the Ephesian elders (Acts 20:17–38) points up the temporary, interim nature of what the apostle was doing there.

Old Testament leaders often followed similar patterns. They were not always happy to give up leadership roles, but knowing this to be God's will for them, they passed on the mantle of authority.

Some of the great women leaders of the Old Testament present helpful images for interim ministry. For example, Deborah (Judges 4, 5) was a judge and a prophet in the time between the invasion of Canaan and the establishment of the monarchy. She provided to the people of God wise counsel, a plan of action, and support in carrying it out. That enabled the people themselves to engage in ministry. Peace in the land was the result of her interim leadership.

Margaret Morris and Joan Mabon, pioneering interim pastors and trainers, have written in the Interim Ministry Network newsletter, *The In-Between Times*:

> Perhaps more than any other, the biblical motif "wilderness" emerges most strongly as the metaphor for a congregation between installed pastors. "Wilderness" is that place of sudden freedom, uncertain leadership, changed relationships, possible deprivation—temptations, hopes, and disappointments. That place where all old fears reappear most threateningly . . . but where all the hopeful futures take on new promise. "Wilderness" becomes a paradigm for the interim time.

Because all congregations must eventually endure something like the wilderness experience, at such times they need leaders who understand the wilderness, persons capable of making it a positive and productive experience.

Experienced, trained interim pastors know that "wilderness" is the setting for storytelling. The interim period is the time for the congregation to retell its own history, to rephrase its ancient stories, to deal with its doubts: "Weren't we better off back there?"

It is time to face the fearsome obstacles that lie beyond the river, to prepare to claim Canaan at the journey's end. Morris and Mabon continue:

> The lively Exodus accounts, the Deuteronomic retelling, even Second Isaiah's gracious return from Exile— all these "wilderness" stories help an unsettled and fearful interim congregation know God's faithfulness, God's steadfast love.

Any congregation alternates between the need for caring nurture and disciplining instruction. At the interim time, those needs often become more pronounced. The need for comforting manna may be painfully overwhelming, while the need for sharp correction may be equally strong, and both comfort and correction can have equal urgency. The issue becomes how to meet these conflicting needs and maintain creative tension between the two. One interim pastor described the prime leadership quality needed for the appropriate balancing of comfort and discipline as a kind of tough love.

Interim ministry is unique, a noteworthy and particular calling. It is generally selective and focused on ministerial tasks that must be accomplished over a limited time. God still calls leaders to short-term special assignments. Interim pastors today are the inheritors of a great calling in a great biblical tradition.

3

Qualifications, Preparation, and Placement

All available ordained ministers are eligible to serve as interim pastors. For pastors in the preretirement years of their ministry, this can become a new career. For those who are retired, interim service can be a satisfying way to use their gifts and experience. For some it will augment slender pensions. Younger persons with little experience may occasionally be invited to serve as interim associate pastors, or as solo interim pastors in smaller churches, but such opportunities are unusual. And rarely will a person with no previous pastoral experience be asked to work as an interim head of staff or as the only interim pastor of a congregation.

Pastors returning from overseas, military or hospital chaplains completing terms of service, or persons making career changes may be well qualified to serve as interim pastors. Many of them will find this a satisfying and practical way to be reintroduced to the parish church in America. All such persons will need some basic training in the theory and practice of interim ministry, however, before they undertake such assignments. It is estimated that there are now hundreds of clergy serving in an interim capacity in Presbyterian churches. They are representative of the best of the pastoral clergy available and a microcosm of the leadership of the church at large.

Qualifications

This ministry requires a considerable degree of flexibility and, whether full-time or part-time, demands good health and a great deal of energy. A list of the desirable personal characteristics of an interim pastor would include the following:

Deep personal faith and commitment to Jesus Christ
and the church

Warm personal qualities

Positive attitude toward the church

A perceptive mind

Common sense

A sense of humor

Ego strength (strong sense of personal worth and
self-assurance)

Self-awareness, especially of one's own working
style

The ability to deal well with stress

Emotional stability

Stable yet flexible personal and family circumstances

Maturity and adaptability for short-term tasks

Mobility, both geographical and psychological

The ability to take risks, tackle the unknown, and
confront problems

Patience and persistence when appropriate

The ability to ask for and accept help

Among the desirable professional qualifications of an interim pastor are the following:

Proven experience as a pastor, or the equivalent

Intentionality (a sense that interim service is a vocational choice, long-term or limited term)

Tolerance for uncertainty in job security and term
of service

Sensitivity to the dynamics of termination, death,
and grief

Interim pastor training or certification

Training or experience in group process

Sensitivity to varied community norms

Thorough knowledge of, and sympathy with, Presbyterian polity, denominational programs, and
linkages

Willingness to work with the presbytery and receive its oversight

Flexibility and adaptability in liturgical practice

The ability to use varied leadership styles in differing situations

Skill in working effectively with the congregation's
other staff, if any

The ability to motivate people

The ability to initiate work quickly and relate
quickly to new people and new situations

The ability to diagnose organizations and develop
strategies for working with them in contract
negotiation; in problem solving, reconciliation,
and healing; and in dealing with conflict openly
and comfortably

It has been suggested that it is desirable, though not essential, for
interim pastors to have financial resources (other than income
from interim service) and a home or retreat to which they can go
during intervals between interim assignments. However, if such
resources are not available, experience indicates that careful planning can usually make up for their lack.

This is a formidable list of desirable characteristics and qualifications; however, few assignments would require that the interim
pastor have every one of the qualities and skills mentioned above.

Consultants to Congregations

Research by the Alban Institute suggests that there are times
when the best course for a congregation is to employ an interim
pastor for the major sustaining tasks of leadership and then to call
in skilled consultants for short-term contract assignments in other
areas such as conflict resolution, management of specific changes
in the congregation, or the development of new programs. Larger
churches and churches experiencing severe conflict are well advised to adopt a team approach during the interim period. Consultants can provide specialized skills to meet particular challenges
and opportunities. Often, engaging a consultant will significantly
reduce the time required to resolve a special problem.

The qualifications for a consultant during an interim time are
virtually the same as for the interim pastor; in addition, the consultant needs special skills and experience in the particular tasks he
or she is expected to do. Consultants who are members of a team
during an interim generally do not conduct worship services. In

that case their preaching and liturgical skills are not a consideration. Neither is it essential that the consultant be trained as an intentional interim pastor, though that would be desirable, as would familiarity with the interim tasks of congregation and pastor alike.

How Does One Become an Interim Pastor?

Prayerful consideration of the possibility of this form of ministry should include study of the scripture and the theological foundations suggested in chapters 2 and 5 and familiarization with the characteristics and skills needed for the task. A talk with someone who is engaged in interim ministry, and with an executive presbyter, will give a better understanding of the work and a feeling as to whether or not one is suited for it.

Training Programs

The oldest and most fully developed training programs for interim pastors are conducted by the Interim Ministry Network. The Alban Institute, a pioneer in the field of specialized training programs for churches and church leaders, gives a number of programs annually in areas of interest to interim pastors or those considering interim service. Addresses for the organizations and institutions mentioned in this manual are listed in the bibliography.

The Presbyterian General Assembly and the Interim Ministry Network offer similar well-developed programs, leading to certification as specialized, qualified, intentional interim pastors. The Presbyterian program includes specific denominational content, whereas the network programs are ecumenical. Both require field experience before certification.

An outline of the Presbyterian certification program can be found in Appendix A. Further information about Presbyterian programs can be obtained from the Associate for Interim Certification and Accreditation, Churchwide Partnerships. The goals of these programs are to help interim pastors in five ways:

1. To know some of the dynamics of termination and institutional grief processes and how to deal with them
2. To be able to assist the local church to use the vacancy situation as a period of significant parish development

3. To know the stages a church goes through while vacant and the roles of consultant and interim pastor in each stage
4. To learn how to relate to a congregation so that its sense of self-determination is enhanced and a minimum of dependency on outside persons and resources is established
5. To be able to help start a creative relationship between the congregation and the new pastor

Additional training programs have been conducted by a number of synods, a few presbyteries, and some seminaries. Interested persons may ask their own presbytery or synod offices for guidance in finding the best places for training. Since most denominational seminaries have continuing education programs, every seminary should consider designing courses that better equip pastors to serve in interim situations.

The Interim Ministry Network publishes a quarterly newsletter, *The In-Between Times*, which provides news about training for interim pastors. Subscriptions to the newsletter are available only to those who join the network.

Placement

The majority of interim assignments are arranged directly through a presbytery office. Churches are often matched with interim pastors who live in the same presbytery or nearby. Pastors desiring to enter interim service should first consult their own presbytery or synod. For those willing to serve beyond their own presbytery, placement services are available through the Associate for Personnel Services, Churchwide Partnerships (see the bibliography for the address).

Interim pastors who wish to use the placement services should notify the General Assembly office each time a new interim assignment is accepted. If subsequent placement is likely to be desired, notice of the pastor's next availability date should be sent to the office (and to selected synod and presbytery offices where the interim would be willing to serve) at least six weeks to two months before the conclusion of the assignment. This is suggested because most sessions, with presbytery assistance, are able to find an interim pastor in about six weeks.

Interim calls are for six months to one year as a rule. Occasionally they are extended. Persons considering careers in interim service face the prospect of frequent moves perhaps over great distances in order to find "steady" employment. Some consider this an advantage and find interim service exciting because it enables them to experience different communities and cultures. One pastor put it this way: "Be an interim and see the nation!"

These realities mean that placement for an interim pastor may be almost as complex as it is for other pastors. Therefore the interim personal information form (PIF) should be as complete as one prepared for an installed position. While most session committees are willing to accept somewhat abbreviated PIFs from interim pastors, short forms are generally more difficult to prepare than complete ones. (When only a few things are to be said, those few must indicate clearly and concisely why one desires to be considered for interim assignments.) Once the PIF is completed, the original copy should be returned to the Associate for Personnel Services, Churchwide Partnerships, the Presbyterian Church (U.S.A.), and copies sent to the interim's own presbytery and synod offices.

Opportunity lists of interim positions are not published by any General Assembly office. Such positions are generally filled so quickly the list would soon be out-of-date. This means that interim pastors need to be both diligent and vigilant in placement matters; otherwise, they may have extended periods without church employment.

The Association of Presbyterian Interim Ministry Specialists (APIMS) does not provide a matching service for interim pastors but does offer a regularly updated list of available interim pastors on the computer network known as Presbynet. This list is called a "closed meeting" since the data it contains are available only to presbytery executives who participate in the Presbynet program. Though limited in its scope, this particular APIMS service is valuable to interim pastors seeking calls and to presbyteries seeking interims. Only those interims who are dues-paying members of APIMS may have their names and a brief résumé on Presbynet.

Continuing Support

Church leaders are becoming more aware of the fact that interims can be of great value to congregations and presbyteries. Yet there is a continuing shortage of trained, intentional interim pastors. More recruitment, training, and placement services are needed to meet the current demands of presbyteries and congregations. If the Presbyterian Church is to move ahead in developing the art of interim ministry, governing bodies and sessions employing interim pastors will need to give more careful attention to the personal needs of interims and their spouses, both as professionals and as private persons. The interim life, after two or three successive interims, can become lonely and at times disorienting. The need for personal support under these conditions is critical.

In response to these needs, a few synods and some presbyteries have organized local gatherings of interim pastors to meet regularly for mutual support and advocacy. Suggestions for developing such programs are found in chapter 9.

How Does a Church Find an Interim Pastor?

Care should be exercised in the selection of interim pastors. It is important to recognize that there are differing responsibilities for the interim, the presbytery, the committee on ministry (COM), the session, and the congregation. When the session decides, in cooperation with COM representatives, that an interim pastor is needed, it must determine what type of service is called for. Maintaining the regular program of the church will be essential. Consideration should also be given to the possible need for grief resolution, conflict management, or healing to reconcile serious differences in the congregation's life. The possibility of development and change in a church's life at this time should be examined as well. Some combination of these tasks will help to define the interim's responsibilities.

A complete but precise position description should be developed by the session and approved by the COM. Only then is a session ready to begin the search. Some presbyteries and synods have lists of available interims and will be glad to consult with sessions about persons who may be a good match for a particular congregation. It is not necessary for the session to prepare a complete church information form in order to get PIFs from the General Assembly office, but it is wise to give as much information as possible about the general situation and the kind of interim desired, including specific skills, the anticipated salary, and the housing arrangements.

When this information is received at the General Assembly office, a search is made among those who have expressed interest in interim service and who seem to have the skills needed. The PIFs of those selected are then sent to the presbytery office or to the persons designated by the COM. Occasionally PIFs are sent directly to the session if the COM approves. One recommended procedure is for the COM to provide the session with several names of persons available, including, when appropriate, those willing to undertake part-time service. In some presbyteries just one pastor's name is suggested to the session seeking an interim. Only if that person is rejected after an interview with the session does the presbytery suggest another name. The session's first contact with a pastor should normally be through the COM. How the session completes its screening and calling of the interim pastor will depend on what advice the presbytery offers. At times this process will parallel what a pastor nominating committee does in calling an installed pastor, except that the interim calling process must be faster and is therefore condensed. While calling an installed pastor may take nine to twelve months, the process of finding an interim usually requires about six weeks, once the session and the presbytery have agreed that an interim should be employed.

Negotiations with a particular pastor concerning the terms of an interim contract are carried out by session representatives in consultation with the presbytery. At this point it may be appropriate to adjust both the position description and the terms of the contract.

In those presbyteries where lists of local interim pastors are not available, the COM or the executive may want to consider procedures for developing and maintaining a list of qualified persons willing to undertake interim ministries. One presbytery executive has suggested the following process:

1.   Pastors already members of the presbytery and willing to consider interim service are asked to submit a one- or two-page PIF or résumé giving their background, skills, and availability.

2.   These pastors are then interviewed by the COM. If the persons interviewed are acceptable to the COM, their names are put into the interim pastor roster of that presbytery.

3.   Pastors who are not members of the presbytery but are

willing to serve there are asked to submit a complete PIF. When the PIF is received, reference checks are made by the COM representative and a telephone interview conducted with the prospective interim pastor before adding that name to the list.

Affirmative Action for Equal Opportunity Employment

A number of presbyteries and synods have used the interim pastor program to promote affirmative action for women in ministry. In several presbyteries and synods, special positions have been established on a three- to five-year plan wherein a woman minister-at-large who is a member of the presbytery or synod staff spends most of her time in service as an interim pastor in individual congregations. Often that pastor is called upon to serve the synod or presbytery in affirmative action work concurrently with interim ministry service. This program has served to introduce some effective women ministers to those congregations and to the presbytery, and the program has been helpful in expanding the opportunities for women to be called as installed pastors.

Some racial-ethnic pastors are also available to be considered as interim pastors and are serving in a few presbyteries. Their number is small, however, and positive steps need to be taken if this situation is to be remedied. Some PIFs for such minority members are available from the General Assembly office.

Presbyteries and synods should continue to implement affirmative action programs of the church-at-large as they expand their own interim rosters and programs. Relevant *Book of Order* sections are G-11.0502f–G-11.0502g.

There are now pastors in almost every affirmative action category—racial-ethnic, female, single, and those with disabilities—pastors who are deserving of special advocacy efforts and who can make a major contribution to the life of a presbytery and its congregations by their special gifts for interim ministry. These pastors are a resource of strength and inspiration that a church neglects to its own considerable loss. Wise church leaders are continuing to make diligent efforts to find and employ these specially gifted pastors in interim ministry. They need and are worthy of widespread affirmative support and encouragement throughout the church.

4

The Work of an Interim Pastor: An Overview

In the first conference for interim pastors sponsored by the Alban Institute in 1975, those present described the following five stages of an interim pastorate: pre-entry, entry, body of the work, exit, and post-termination.

Stages of an Interim Pastorate

Stage 1: Pre-entry
Average time: 3 days to 4 weeks

Certain things need to occur before the interim pastor has contact with the congregation. Presbytery policy about the work of the interim should be clarified. He or she needs to develop a trust relationship with the presbytery executive and/or the committee on ministry (COM) chairperson or representative. The interim pastor, the executive, and any consultants involved need to know and support each other effectively. The interim should be learning as much as possible about the church and then consider thoughtfully how to get in, be there, and, at the right time, get out.

The presbytery representative, as well as the session, should share with the interim pastor any specific expectations or problems that need to be dealt with during the interim time. Guidance should be given as to what should have immediate attention, since there will be only limited time to deal with any issue. The interim should look upon such guidance as helpful and in no sense a threat to the ministry to be performed.

The relationship between the interim pastor and the COM and between the interim pastor and the session is a reciprocal one. In the pre-entry stage, each party makes clear what is expected of the other. Key questions to be answered include the following: How does the presbytery understand this congregation? What are its strengths, its problems, its needs? What are its opportunities now?

The session and the COM together should have a clear understanding of who will be responsible for each part of the pre-entry and entry processes. Questions that need to be answered include the following: Who will interpret the concept of the interim pastorate to the congregation? Who will explain what the interim does and does *not* do, how the interim is selected, and how long the interim will stay? The congregation should be informed as to the nature of the covenant or contract (including the job description) that has been agreed upon.

Publicity about the coming of the interim pastor, including some background, should be shared with the community as well as the congregation. This will let people know that things are well in hand and are moving forward.

Stage 2: Entry
Average time: 3 or 4 weeks

Entry involves contract negotiations with the presbytery, the COM, and the session. It demands that the interim pastor, the session, and the presbytery have a clear understanding about the character of this relationship. Such understanding begins with study of the *Book of Order* references in G-14.0513b–G-14.0513c. Primary contracting is usually done between the interim and the session, with the presbytery's advice and counsel. The presbytery executive and/or representatives from the COM may meet with representatives of the session and perhaps with the interim to develop a concise statement about the tasks to be accomplished during the interim period by the interim pastor, the session, and others in the congregation or presbytery.

Important features of the congregation's life need to be identified and clear, short-term key objectives of the interim pastor's work described in a carefully worded position description. This helps to establish trust between the interim, the session, and the congregation and makes the special goals of interim ministry easier to achieve. A contract dealing with salary, length of term, benefits, and the like is also essential. Some prefer to call this agreement a covenant rather than a contract. A contract between Christians becomes a covenant when it is based on faith, guided by the Spirit of God, and there is giving and receiving for mutual benefit among all parties. From another perspective, the covenant is part of the "psychological contract" that develops between the session, the congregation, the presbytery, and the interim pastor. This kind of covenanting, whether formal or informal, occurs and reoccurs continually as the interim meets different groups and individuals in the congregation.

An initial part of the entry will be orientation of the interim pastor to the congregation and its history, to the community and its essential elements, and to the presbytery and its work. The presbytery executive or associate, the COM, or some other committee or individual should make sure this orientation is adequate, prompt, and quickly completed.

The skilled interim pastor will take the first few weeks of an interim assignment to get a full perspective on the situation and to develop a list of objectives for this particular ministry. The list will be reviewed with the session and the presbytery to be sure it is valid and realistic. Such a list must be limited. What is really possible in the time available for this ministry?

All the objectives should be measurable, ranked, and weighted so that the interim pastor has a clear idea of what comes first and what is most critical. Some of the most significant tasks are not necessarily the ones that should be addressed first. The list will not be complete until the interim and the session together decide exactly who will perform what tasks. A specific person or group should be responsible for each objective and a report and follow-up plan adopted early in the entry stage.

Covenanting Service or Service of Recognition

The presbytery will want to recognize the significance of this new interim relationship by sharing leadership in a special worship service that will emphasize the covenantal nature of this unique call and will involve the entire congregation in the covenant. Such a service can be designed both to inform and to inspire the congregation, the session, and the interim pastor. There may also be some brief, meaningful recognition of and prayer for the new interim at a meeting of the presbytery. A suggested liturgy for this purpose is in Appendix D of this manual.

Staff Interviews

The interim should conduct interviews of all paid staff and key volunteers, any persons with specific and significant roles in the congregation: clergy, music director, administrative support, and custodians. All need time to meet with the new interim pastor. These conversations should be more than brief formalities.

Church officers, moderators, chairpersons, and other church leaders should be on this list of early introductions, with substantive conversations included in the initial meetings or soon thereafter. Church school leaders and teachers might also be on this list. All these persons will have information that can be of real value to the interim in this stage. The interim pastor may want to ask them some of these questions:

> How do these persons see their positions and tasks?
> What are their needs and their opportunities?
> How can they and the interim pastor mutually support one another in their work together?

Speedy entry is essential. Social occasions are helpful. Early meetings of all the church boards offer the interim excellent times to get better acquainted. The sooner the interim pastor can call the church officers by their first names, the easier the work will be.

An Entry Checklist

The following list is only suggestive, and its use will vary from church to church and from pastor to pastor. Still, it should be reviewed early in the entry process.

> What major program events are coming up?
> Does this church usually follow the Christian liturgical calendar?
> Is there a local church calendar?
> What are this congregation's most important customs, holidays, and annual events?
> What individuals and families will need pastoral attention during the first two or three weeks?
> Is there a system for notifying the interim pastor of pastoral care needs? (If there is no such system, one should be established.)

Where are the hospitals most commonly used by
church members?

Where can the interim find a map of the community?

Where are the funeral homes and what does the
interim need to know about local funeral directors?

Does the session have a policy about funerals held
in the church building?

What are this congregation's policies and practices
regarding weddings, baptisms, and funerals, the
use of the building, and church equipment?

Are those policies different for outside organizations and individuals?

What ecumenical relationships does the congregation maintain?

Is there a local ministers' association or a council of
churches?

What community relationships are important to
the church?

In this early stage the interim pastor will also want to study some
of the church records: a current membership list and a church directory (especially a recent picture directory), session records and
minutes, personnel policies, the church budget and financial reports, any recent self-study, and lists of church organizations and
their officers. When the church information form is complete, the
interim pastor should have a copy (unless that is contrary to the
presbytery's policy).

Stage 3: The Body of the Work
Average time: 4 to 10 months

During this period the interim pastor focuses on providing the
pastoral functions the congregation requires, maintaining and
strengthening its worship and nurture. Special opportunities are
available to deal with grief and termination, with trust, with congregational identity, and with expectations for the future. All these
issues can be handled as part of the ordinary pastoral functions of
an interim rather than as something "new." The interim's sensitivity to these dimensions of congregational life will help the congregation to reflect on what is happening, what has happened, and

what should happen, thus guiding the congregation in its continuing development.

A major part of the interim pastor's time and energy during this middle period will be invested in guiding the congregation in its work on its five developmental tasks (to be discussed in chapter 5); parallel to these are the five process tasks of the interim pastor (discussed in chapter 6). The interim, the session, and the entire congregation should understand that they all have much more to do than simply marking time until the pastor nominating committee (PNC) completes its search.

Usually it is during this middle stage that the search for the next installed pastor begins. If the interim pastor is to have any relationship to the PNC, it must be carefully defined ahead of time. Some COMs prefer that the interim not work with the PNC. Still, the interim pastor and the session have some responsibility to make sure that at least the outline of the search process is clearly communicated to the congregation. The COM representative can define how this is to be done. Sometimes the interim can identify information that should be passed on to the COM to aid them in advising the PNC or prospective candidates for the pulpit. Whatever the COM requires, the interim pastor will always serve as a key member of a team that includes the session, the congregation, the COM, the presbytery, and the PNC.

While integrity and dependability are essential qualities of interim pastors, flexibility is also required. Throughout every interim assignment, objectives, plans, and tasks agreed upon ought to be open to adjustment and renegotiation if circumstances change. Agreements ought not to be altered, however, unless there are significant unexpected developments and there is general agreement.

Styles and Methods of Leadership

There are three leadership styles that can be useful during the interim period:

1. **Consultative**—Decisions are made by the interim pastor after consultation with appropriate groups.
2. **Collegial or Participatory**—Decisions are made jointly by groups or key leaders and the interim pastor.
3. **Directive**—The interim pastor takes a strong hand and directs groups in the decision-making process.

The collegial or participatory style is often the one most effectively used, though the pastor's style may vary according to the particular purpose, the specific tasks at hand, and the desired results. In troubled congregations a major part of the problem sometimes has been the leadership style of the pastor. Many pastors are either too laissez-faire or too authoritarian. Rarely is either of those styles what the congregation wants, especially in an interim period, needing instead the development of more lay leaders. The collegial or participatory style generally best serves that goal.

In working with troubled congregations, however, the interim pastor may find that a strongly confrontational or directive style will get to the heart of the congregation's problems more quickly than the consultative method. Because the interim is active in one congregation for a relatively short time, a direct, authoritative, possibly abrasive management approach will often get a job done more rapidly.

Other occasions will demand other styles of leadership. Working with small groups not directly responsible for decision making in the church may call for a more collegial style. Many one-to-one relationships require special counseling methods and listening skills. The wise and experienced interim will usually be in command of a variety of styles for working with a congregation and will adapt the style to the group, the individual, or the situation.

Once the first excitement of a new face and a new voice in the pulpit has passed, there may be a tendency in the congregation to rest on its oars and drift leisurely down the stream until the new pilot appears. The interim pastor needs to be alert to this tendency, to understand why it happens, and to know what to do about it. The desired response from the congregation is to ensure that when the new pastor arrives, the congregation will be moving full speed ahead, under their own energy and leadership, ready to enter into a new relationship, in a new era, under a new, eagerly welcomed pastor.

During this third stage of the work there should be a midterm assessment of how the interim work is going. Together, the interim pastor and the session should look at what progress the congregation and the session are making on the five developmental tasks and how the interim is doing on the process tasks. Other elements of church life will also need review. Midcourse corrections may be called for. Individuals or groups may need encouragement or guidance. Such a review will help to energize everyone so they can continue to serve in a focused way at full capacity.

Stage 4: Exit
Average time: 1 or 2 months

In the period of termination, the search process concludes and a new pastor is elected. The termination phase is used to assist the congregation in doing its grief work about the interim pastor's leaving—and the previous pastor's leaving, too, if that still needs work. Then the congregation is free to enter a healthy relationship with the new pastor. The interim works to build anticipation for the coming of the new pastor, help the congregation clarify its expectations, and deal with any possible anxiety. The exit stage should be a time of real celebration for everyone for at least two reasons: first, because a new pastor, the right pastor, is coming; second, because the interim tasks belonging to the congregation and to the interim pastor have all been successfully completed.

Saying Good-bye and Meaning It!

The effective interim pastor's termination process begins at the time of the first conversation with the session and goes into full swing on arriving to begin work in the church. It must be clear from the beginning that this is an *interim* assignment. Building a strategy for termination should be part of the original conversation with the COM and with the session. In every case, the planning should relate to one of the chief goals of both the interim and the congregation: to prepare the way for the new pastor and for a new chapter in the life of the congregation. The termination strategy can take a variety of forms. The worship service, Bible study and other programs, even pastoral calling can be opportunities for preparing the way for the one who is to come. The first sermon the interim preaches, for example, ought to say both "hello" and "good-bye."

The church staff will also need to be prepared for the coming of the new pastor. Discussion with the session or the personnel committee can develop ways to do this.

The wise interim pastor can build enthusiasm in the congregation over the coming of the new pastor. Sermons, teaching, even casual conversations can help alleviate congregational impatience and heighten healthy expectations. The interim can also warn against expecting too much too soon. One experienced pastor said to the congregation toward the end of the interim, "Remember this: You cannot expect your new pastor to work the way I have here. Your next pastor will be installed and therefore will have a different situation with different relationships. She will need to work in a different way." Another said, "I have had forty years' experience in ministry. Your new pastor has had only four years since seminary. Do not expect him to act, work, or perform in the way I have."

Many interim pastors are older and more secure than some installed pastors. They may appear more confident and make a better impression on the congregation. Depending on the particular interim pastorate, the interim often will not get beyond the honeymoon stage in the relationship, so both the interim pastor and the congregation will have unreal assessments of each other. As part of the preparation for the next pastor, congregations and interim pastors need to understand this dynamic of most interim relationships. Making the future vital and rewarding is as much the task of the officers and members of the congregation as it is of the new pastor.

Concluding Worship Services

In the last few weeks the interim may want to give a "state of the church" report to the congregation or to the session, perhaps as part of a sermon at Sunday worship or at some other time. Another theme for one of the last Sundays might be "How to treat your new pastor."

The final worship service should include some kind of termination ceremony with prayers for the congregation, its leaders, and its new pastor. The liturgy and the sermon should emphasize thanksgiving and celebration for all that has been and for what is to come. Several interims have written their own liturgies of farewell. The session's worship committee can use this opportunity to help the congregation to complete its work on the fifth developmental task: commitment to new leadership and a new future (see chapter 5). One purpose of this occasion would be to express appreciation for the work of the interim and to offer prayers for the fruitfulness of that pastor's next ministry.

Stage 5: Post-Termination
Average time: 1 to 4 weeks

A careful review of the whole interim experience is important to determine whether the desired objectives were achieved. Reflection and evaluation by presbytery executives, congregational groups, and the interim pastor can add a useful dimension to everyone's understanding of what happened. Evaluation of the interim's work by the session and a similar review of the work of the session and congregation by the interim pastor should be the minimum requested by the presbytery.

"There is an element of mystery in ministry, and the Holy Spirit does not always act through persons in predictable ways," one interim pastor wrote. The quality of the spiritual life is beyond measurement, and yet that may be the most important factor in the pastor's impact upon a congregation. Even though much of ministry deals with intangibles, there is still a great deal that can be clearly evaluated. A review and analysis of the work done, the work not done, and consequent results ought to be part of the closing days and the follow-up for every interim pastor. The COM should be sure that such a review takes place.

How will such evaluations be used? The results are shared with all persons who participate in the evaluation. The interim pastor will grow from every such experience, learning how to do a better job next time. And while individual elders may never again serve as members of the session during an interim period, their continuing service to the congregation will be enriched by completing the interim evaluation.

5

The Congregation's
Five Developmental Tasks

The congregation has its own tasks to work on during the time the nominating committee is seeking a new pastor, but most congregations are not fully aware of them. They are therefore unlikely to complete them satisfactorily without some guidance.

The five tasks have been named as follows: (1) coming to terms with history, (2) discovering a new identity, (3) allowing and empowering new leaders, (4) renewing denominational linkages, and (5) committing to new leadership and a new future. These tasks are called *developmental* to indicate that they are areas in which the congregation needs to *develop* greater maturity in self-understanding and greater skill in doing what needs to be done. In this way the congregation will be able to take full advantage of the opportunity the interim period offers to prepare itself to achieve the aims and goals Christ has set before these disciples in this church.

Some of these special tasks are, in part, the kinds of things people or organizations may do naturally, without encouragement or guidance, when they face significant losses or changes in their community or individual lives. Experience with churches, however, indicates that these matters are important enough to require special attention during the interim period if the congregation is to move successfully through this time and into a new life under a new installed pastor. If these tasks are not addressed and adequately completed during the interim period, the next installed pastor will need to guide the congregation in completing this work. His or her start-up period will thus be extended, and the energy of both pastor and officers will be directed to tasks that could better have been completed during the interim.

While there may be considerable variety in the way the tasks are addressed and in the results achieved, the skilled interim pastor should understand the church's five tasks and know how to guide and encourage the congregation in its work on them. (In addition to the congregation's five developmental tasks, David R. Sawyer, a consultant in church organization and systems and an experienced interim pastor, has written that there is a related series of five process tasks for the interim pastor, the interim executive, or other interim leader. We shall consider Sawyer's list of process tasks in chapter 6.)

Awareness of the congregation's developmental tasks grew out of a gathering of interim pastors and other church leaders convened by the Alban Institute in St. Louis in the mid-1970s. Loren Mead, founder of the Alban Institute, was present and was the first to describe the tasks and their significance to congregations in transitional times. He published these ideas in a helpful monograph, *The Developmental Tasks of the Parish in Search of a Pastor*, shortly after the St. Louis conference. Later he expanded this concept in the book *Critical Moment of Ministry: A Change of Pastors*, which was published by the Alban Institute. The fourth chapter of that book is devoted entirely to a consideration of the five developmental tasks.

Why are these tasks best addressed during a time of transition? Organizations, like individuals, resist change, especially significant changes such as these tasks may suggest. Because losing a pastor is a major change in the life of any congregation, one could reason that it would be best to allow the congregation to deal carefully with that loss before asking them to make any additional changes. However, if the five tasks are *not* completed during the interim, many in the congregation are likely to expect that the next chapter in their church's life will be like the one just past. That can mean serious trouble for the new pastor. Working on the five tasks is usually the best way to promote the conscious and healthy dealing with denial, grieving, healing, and rebuilding that a change in pastors requires. As we examine these tasks more closely, we will discover that each one of them can be most effectively addressed during a time of change and transition—that is, during the interim between installed pastors.

The first four of the tasks are not necessarily sequential, and the order in which they are undertaken may vary widely from place to place and time to time. In fact, if a particular session or congregation has the needed leadership resources, it is possible for that congregation to work on more than one of these tasks simultaneously. In most cases, however, such a plan of action would not be desirable. It is usually wise to begin with the first task, coming to terms with history. It is a healthy way to deal with loss of a beloved pastor or with the uncertainty and possible guilt and conflict that can follow the involuntary termination of a pastor.

One interim pastor says she finds that the five tasks are interactive in nature and that energy, inspiration, focus, and attention should flow from one task to another and back again throughout the entire time of the interim experience. For example, the third task, allowing and empowering new leaders, is one important element in completing the second task, discovering a new identity, and vice versa.

Not all these tasks will take an equal amount of time or energy in every congregation. Discovering a new identity can be relatively easy in some congregations, while in others it may require major effort. In some churches the established leaders may not allow the development of any new leadership during the interim time, yet elsewhere such changes will come easily.

The American Baptist Ministers-at-Large Program in Valley Forge, Pennsylvania, has published a series of workshop guides that cover each of the five tasks. They are useful resources for every interim pastor to carry from church to church. The workshops are designed in such a way that they can be used individually or in a series. Such studies would be fresh and singularly timely for the adult education class of a church in transition, and they need not be conducted solely by the interim pastor.

The rest of this chapter is devoted to suggestions for the congregation's work on each of the five tasks.

Coming to Terms with History

Memory is one of God's greatest gifts to humankind. Properly used, memory enables a person or a community to become whole, to mature, and to make wise use of the lessons of experience. The broader and deeper the memory becomes, the more competent and successful that person or community will become, provided they have learned how to employ memories productively. Scripture is full of stories to emphasize the importance of remembering history for generations. A great deal of the strength of Israel's faith, and of our Christian faith, is in large part sustained by the stories faithful people tell and retell to one another and to their children. When Joshua crossed the Jordan, he commanded twelve men to take up stones from the river and build a memorial in Gilgal. Then Joshua said, "When your children ask in time to come, 'What do those stones mean to you?' then you shall tell them. . . . So these stones shall be to the Israelites a memorial forever" (Josh. 4:6–7).

The earliest generations of Christian churches were also inspired by the retelling of the stories of the heroes of the faith. The Letter to the Hebrews, chapter 11, greatly challenges all Christians, as do the opening verses of chapter 12: "Therefore, since we are surrounded by so great a cloud of witnesses . . . let us run with perseverance the race that is set before us, looking to Jesus the pioneer and perfecter of our faith" (Heb. 12:1–2). Church people will respond warmly when they are led to see the scriptural models and the theological significance of this first task. During the interim time, when many congregations feel lost and leaderless, the strength and courage these texts give can help generate the energy people need to move forward and review their own congregation's history.

There will be different memories and different perspectives on the same memories. Some will recall only "the good old days," while others think just of the bad times. Even if a congregation's history reveals great difficulty, the people still can be encouraged to say, "Look, our parents and grandparents survived. We'll make it too, by God's grace!" And when the stories they can recall are happy ones, the congregation gains both joy and hope. People are always better off when they deal honestly and openly with their history. That is how we learn to "run with perseverance the race that is set before us." The important consideration is to come to terms with history, to review it, and to acknowledge it, beauty and blemishes alike. Then, having acknowledged the past, we may consider what it means for the present and how it can be understood to help to shape the future productively. The time this will take is always a wise investment.

A direct approach to this task would be to ask one of the members to write a history of the church, a plan especially appropriate if the congregation is approaching a major anniversary. Such a history might be published as a book, or serialized in the church newsletter, or used in church school classes. If there are any records of earlier anniversary celebrations, they would prove useful in working on this task. Some churches have presented dramatizations of their history or called attention to memorial windows, furniture, or plaques. If there is a "rogues' gallery"—portraits of former pastors—somewhere in the church, a review or celebration of those individuals might be a positive step. If such a collection does not exist, the interim pastor may suggest developing something of the sort.

As for preaching, the interim pastor should think, while preparing the sermon or the liturgy for worship, "Can this text help the congregation to do its work on one or more of these developmental tasks?" The interim who has the tasks well in mind will be surprised by how often one of them can be addressed through preaching, in prayers, in the choice of hymns, or in other parts of worship.

In summary, the goal in dealing with the congregation's history is to guard the people from any extreme reactions to their history, to acknowledge past difficulties as times of testing that have strengthened the church to meet today's challenges, to focus most on proud moments in the past and on current strengths of the church, and to encourage both the session and the congregation to dream an inspiring, satisfying, achievable future. To do this well, the interim pastor should have, and should encourage in the congregation, both a sense of perspective and a sense of humor. Do not belabor their history; it can be overdone. Remember, there are four other developmental tasks to be worked on as well.

Discovering a New Identity

The New Year Festival of the Hebrew people in the Old Testament often included the reading or singing of Psalm 96, "O sing to the Lord a new song. . . . Tell of his salvation from day to day. Declare his glory among the nations" (Ps. 96:1–3). This festival acknowledged the renewal of the covenant between God and the creation and with the people of Israel. The covenant served as the foundation for the life of Israel, and the people responded annually by singing a new song that grew out of their common memory of God's saving acts. The church today, like Israel and the New Testament church, should regularly reaffirm the new covenant. Since this new covenant is at the heart of the church's life, it is therefore a key element in its identity. This psalm, or similar passages from scripture, can help the congregation to reaffirm the covenant and appreciate the need for a new identity, if the church is to continue to minister to a changing community. From that beginning, the discovery of other facets of a new identity will naturally flow. Each generation is called to sing its own "new song."

Congregations often describe their history in terms of the pastors who served them. This common reality has significant implications. First, when the pastor leaves, whatever the reason for the departure, such a church has lost its focal point and may be both confused and despondent. Members of the congregation need to be led to understand that their identity as a church is not tied to any one human being but includes everyone who is a part of the church family. The pastor is only a part of their history. It is not Jesus Christ who has left the church, just the former pastor. The interim will want to be sensitive and considerate about when and how to make such statements, especially while the congregation is still mourning their loss. In such cases, finding a new identity is especially critical. Otherwise the congregation may sink into depression.

When there is a real vacuum in leadership and a loss of focus, the time of a pastoral vacancy is full of opportunity. It is a time for creating a new self-understanding. A self-study—or mission study, as it may be called—is of great importance. If it includes statistical, practical, and spiritual dimensions, such a study can provide a useful foundation on which to build a new structure to support new life in the congregation.

A former pastor may not be the focal point of a church's identity. Other factors may determine the congregation's nature and self-image. Longtime members, an inner circle of devoted church officers, established traditions for worship, for educational programs, and for the congregation's social activities—all these can combine to give a congregation a strong identity. Such an identity may or may not be right for the next chapter of this church's life. The old nature and self-image need to be reexamined to see if they are valid for the future.

Another consideration is the image the church has in the community, for that image will subtly interact with the church's self-image. Many churches have no clear picture of what their non-Presbyterian neighbors think of them. Now is the time to explore this question too.

The self-study offers a well-defined opportunity for the congregation to look not only at itself but at the challenges of the community it serves. Often a community changes radically while the church itself is static. Members may be unaware of what has happened to people and institutions in their own neighborhood.

The presbytery may require that a congregation complete a self-study of some kind before it is allowed to elect a pastor nominating committee (PNC). If so, some key questions to ask are the following: Does the presbytery have a prescribed plan for conducting this study? When should it be done? Will the interim pastor be involved in any way? Some presbyteries discourage any involvement by the interim in a congregation's self-study. If the interim is serving in a presbytery with no specific plan for such a study, he or she should be ready with suggestions for the session as to why and how this should be done. Resources are listed in the bibliography for guidance in this task.

Changing pastors gives a church many precious opportunities. Among these, perhaps the chief one is the opportunity to discover a new identity that fits the realities and the new challenges in its ministry.

Allowing and Empowering
New Leaders

Awe at the power of God is universal in the scriptures, which both begin and end with statements describing the nature of God's power. Genesis reads, "In the beginning when God created the heavens and the earth," and we find in those words an introduction to the unlimited power of the omnipotent creator God. In the Gospel we find Jesus' words, "All authority [power] in heaven and on earth has been given to me" (Matt. 28:18), and John's message, "He was in the world, and . . . to all who received him, who believed in his name, he gave power" (John 1:10, 12).

When Christian leaders have power in the church or in any other sphere of life, it is derived from God in Christ and is to be exercised reverently, purposefully, and lovingly for Christ's purposes in the church and in the world. But God has given us freedom to use power for our own selfish ends. Church people can be as guilty of abuses of power as any others. Especially during the interim time, a congregation needs to examine the nature of power, how it is used and how it ought to be used.

Leadership changes are likely to follow naturally from the congregation's work on the preceding task, discovering a new identity. Electing new church officers, however, does not itself necessarily mean a real shift of power, or a genuine leadership change, or a new identity for the congregation. Church leaders who hold no office in the congregation may still have a great deal of influence.

Individuals get or are given power to lead a congregation in a variety of ways. There are also several kinds of power, and different ways power may be used. An understanding of the nature of power and its uses will be of real value to the interim pastor and to lay leaders.

Roy Oswald, author, trainer, and consultant with the Alban Institute for a number of years, has written a concise analysis of both personal and corporate power as it is expressed in a congregation. He suggests there are at least four power "currencies" in a church: structural, reputational, coalitional, and communicational.

1. **Structural power**—Comes from holding an official position in the congregation or perhaps from some unofficial yet influential position in the organization.
2. **Reputational power**—Comes from the image a person has in the church, usually as a result of past accomplishments, social position, or family connections; it may also be derived from personal talents or gifts.
3. **Coalitional power**—Develops when one person unites with others of like purposes and interests to achieve common goals.
4. **Communicational power**—Held by people who have information and know when and how to share it effectively.

An appreciation of these different forms of power and their uses will help both the interim pastor and key congregational leaders in carrying on the task of encouraging new leadership while working with present leaders and power coalitions.

In terms of structural and coalitional power, several kinds of change may be observed during an interim. Some people will move out of leadership roles because they carried a heavy load under the previous pastor and now want less responsibility. The pastor's departure may seem a good time to give up much or all of their service to the church. Others who may have had some difficulty in working with the previous pastor are ready to move back into leadership positions, either eagerly and aggressively or tentatively and hesitantly. Jan Chartier, a Baptist interim pastor, in a workshop guide on "Shifts of Power," suggests there may be a group that often develops naturally that can be called the "emergency squad." They are persons willing to assume temporary leadership during the interim period. There are others, however, who shift into neutral and wait to see what is going to happen. Still others, dropouts in the previous era, may now return to leadership roles. It will be difficult, at first, for the interim pastor to identify these different individuals, but session members probably can sort them out. Doing so could be of real value in guiding the congregation as it works on this third task. A workshop on "Shifts of Power"—for the session, for all church officers, or for members of the congregation's nominating committee (not the PNC)—might be very useful.

The presbytery or the synod may have leadership resources or programs and services that will assist the congregation in taking a look at its power structure and its practices in the use or abuse of power. If that is not the case, the interim may want to encourage the presbytery to conduct workshops or programs that will help all churches in the presbytery that are presently seeking pastors.

Renewing Denominational Linkages

In times of crisis and uncertainty, God's people have found strong, renewing power in remembering their heritage in faith. "Look to the rock from which you were hewn," Isaiah wrote, "and to the quarry from which you were dug. Look to Abraham your father and to Sarah who bore you" (Isa. 51:1–2). Presbyterians in America often find a sense of pride and a source of strength when they review the role of their spiritual ancestors in the American Revolution, or when they study the Long Parliament and the Westminster Assembly from which grew the Westminster Confession of Faith in England, or when they claim the heritage of John Calvin, John Knox, or John Witherspoon. They have often celebrated the worldwide impact of their overseas mission outreach and the precedent-setting influence of their home mission policies and programs. Presbyterians are justifiably proud of their leadership in higher education throughout America, having founded some of the first and finest colleges and universities our nation knows.

In more recent years, Presbyterians have been prominent among leaders of the civil rights movement and the social justice programs for the poor and oppressed, both in America and beyond our shores and borders. All this history is part of the "rock from which [we] were hewn" and gives us occasion to celebrate the traditions that are ours. As the interim pastor guides the congregation in its work on the first developmental task, coming to terms with history, the fourth task can provide depth and breadth to a developing picture of the denominational church.

Presbyterians can find wisdom and strength in our *Book of Confessions*, our 1990 Presbyterian *Hymnal* (and the old ones too), and in our new *Book of Common Worship*. Our excellent curriculum and other fine program resources and publications from the General Assembly offices will also help to build knowledge and pride in our heritage as Presbyterians. These are some of the treasures from which the interim pastor can create sermons, programs, prayers, and leadership ideas and by means of which the congregation can renew their links to their Presbyterian heritage.

Help for the Pastor Nominating Committee

The most obvious help from the denomination comes to the church during the interim time in the form of guidance and resources for the PNC. Each of the governing bodies provides some services to the PNC. The presbytery, through the committee on ministry, offers training and guidance to the PNC. The synod may offer face-to-face opportunities, where the PNC can meet a number of likely candidates for the pastoral position. And the General Assembly provides a structure for the search process through publications, papers, and personnel-matching resources. The whole congregation should be informed as to how our denominational connections make it easier for the PNC to do its work well.

Resources of the General Assembly

Among the printed resources that the interim pastor can employ in the work on this fourth task is the *General Assembly Program Calendar*, which should be made available to all members of

the church staff and to as many lay leaders as possible, both volunteer and paid, full-time and part-time. *The Mission Yearbook for
Prayer and Study* will also produce dividends in many unexpected
ways when it is used in classes, programs, and worship services
large and small. Both of these, as well as a host of other print, au-
dio, and video materials are available by a simple phone call or a
note to the denomination's headquarters or possibly may be bor-
rowed from the presbytery or synod office.

There are human resources available, too. The presbytery
staff and others in the presbytery, both clergy and lay leaders,
should be invited to appear at worship, in meetings and classes,
and at receptions and suppers. Christian leaders from other nations, missionaries and fraternal workers, refugees, and international students will further enlarge the congregation's understanding of the nature and extent of our denomination's
outreach into the world and the response that has come back to
us as a result of our sharing of Christ's good news to the ends of
the earth.

Encouraging elders, deacons, and other church members to
participate in the activities of the presbytery, the synod, and the
General Assembly is another way to strengthen ties to the larger
church. It may have been many months or even years since the
congregation has been represented by an elder delegate or elder
commissioner at a presbytery meeting. The elders who attend
presbytery meetings should be given a place on the docket of the
next session meeting to report their reflections on what happened
there.

The Roots of Our Connectionalism

A review of the Acts of the Apostles, of the missionary journeys
of Paul and Barnabas and Silas, a study of the significance of the
first Council at Jerusalem in Acts 15, and a look at Paul's urging
offerings for "the saints at Jerusalem" (Rom. 15:26; 1 Cor. 16:1,
3)—all this will give the congregation a new appreciation of the
connectional church. Our New Testament heritage gives us a
model that directs us to honor these connections in our denomination and in the ecumenical church. The congregation that
works faithfully at both understanding and renewing its denominational linkages during the interim time will be immeasurably
strengthened for years to come.

Commitment to New Leadership and a New Future

The congregation has finished its interim developmental tasks only when it is genuinely ready to make a commitment to new leadership and a new future. Like a number of the other developmental tasks, this last task relates to each of the others. Work done on the first four tasks contributes to the accomplishment of the fifth.

Jesus often used the analogy of a wedding to suggest the joy that comes from entering the new life he promised to his disciples. John the Baptist also spoke of the joy in preparation and celebration of a wedding (John 3:28–29). The interim pastor can use this reference to help the congregation to compare welcoming a new pastor to a joyful wedding that requires much preparation. The effective interim shares the joy of the congregation and models the humility of John the Baptist. He or she will step into the background with a feeling of happiness for the congregation and for the new pastor.

Given the fact that the interim pastor may be experiencing the personal pains of leave-taking from people who not long ago were strangers but are now good friends, sharing the joyful spirit of a wedding ceremony may not be easy. That is the nature, however, of much interim ministry. It is a blend of contradictions and paradoxes. That is part of what makes interim service such a challenge and yet so richly rewarding to those who take it up "not to be served, but to serve."

Part of the congregation's readiness to say hello to their new pastor depends on their having said good-bye to the interim pastor (and all previous pastors). If necessary, the interim needs to take the initiative by reminding the session (or the clerk) that they should plan a significant farewell. This should be a celebration of such a nature that everyone will know they have said their good-byes and that the interim pastor has truly left the church and the community.

But what about commitment to a "new future"? How much can or should an interim pastor do to lead or assist a session or a congregation in defining and getting ready for new tasks and new forms of ministry and mission? If the session and the congregation have completed their work on the first four developmental tasks, they will be ready for their new future.

The five developmental tasks are the heart of the matter, both for the session and for the congregation, during the in-between time when there is no installed pastor. Each task will need attention at some point during the interim period. Some tasks can be profitably addressed frequently or occasionally, while others may need work only once. Since there are many ways to accomplish each of them, perhaps the greatest thing the interim pastor can do is to inspire the creativity of all in the congregation so they may be innovative and relevant in their work on these tasks. What the session and the congregation need most is a deep determination to do each part of this job thoroughly, demonstrating the essential qualities of every faithful Christian leader, including a sense of humor, a well of sympathy and compassion, and endless patience.

6

The Interim Pastor's
Five Process Tasks

David R. Sawyer, interim pastor and church consultant, has
suggested that the five developmental tasks of the interim congregation have a parallel in five other tasks that are the unique and
individual responsibility of the interim pastor. He calls these
"process tasks" since they focus on "processes of a human system,
such as patterns of organization and behavior, relationships, communication, and decision-making." In a two-part article, "The
Process Tasks of the Interim Leader," published in 1994 in the *In-
Between Times* (the newsletter of the Interim Ministry Network),
Sawyer listed these tasks as: (1) joining the system, (2) analyzing
the organization as a system, (3) connecting with the denomination, (4) focusing and assuming responsibility, and (5) exiting and
evaluating.

These process tasks are helpful ways to understand and organize the tasks that are the particular personal responsibility of the
interim pastor and are not to be confused with what may be called
the program tasks of the interim pastor (such things as preaching,
teaching, pastoral care, and leadership development). Program
tasks involve the same kinds of responsibilities installed pastors
must undertake. For the interim pastor they require a somewhat
different approach, and they are not the subject of this chapter.

Students of interim ministry have pointed out that a compari-
son of the five developmental tasks of the congregation and the
five process tasks of the interim pastor reveal some similarities and
some interesting contrasts.

Both sets of tasks start with one that obviously belongs at the
beginning of the interim experience, both for the congregation
and for the pastor. By contrast, however, we find that there is generally a significant difference between the emotional tone of the

congregation and that of the interim pastor as they work on their first tasks. For the congregation, coming to terms with history often starts as a disheartening experience in which people deal with their sadness over the loss of a former pastor. There may be also a deeper grief, even anger, if there has been any kind of misconduct by the former pastor (especially sexual misconduct). For the interim, however, the excitement of joining a new and challenging system can be exhilarating just at the time when the congregation may be feeling anxious and despondent, when their critical needs are for comfort and courage rather than for celebration.

Both developmental and process tasks conclude with one that cannot be completed until the search committee is close to finding its candidate for the installed position. For the congregation, the fifth task is committing to new leadership and a new future; for the interim pastor, the fifth task is exiting and evaluating. Here again the emotions of the congregation and the interim may well be at opposite poles. The congregation is excited and happy to know that they will soon have a new pastor, while the interim is probably experiencing some sadness as this interim pastorate is about to end. Circumstances will vary, but in general the tendency is for congregation and pastor to be at opposite extremes of the emotional scale at both the beginning and the end of the interim period.

Process tasks two, three, and four are less time-oriented. As noted in chapter 5, they can be addressed concurrently or sequentially. Analyzing the organization, connecting with the denomination, focusing and assuming responsibility—all can be worked on at any time after a satisfactory entry.

Parallels and contrasts between the interim pastor's work and the congregation's work call for sensitivity and skill every step of the way. A thorough understanding and appreciation of both will help the interim choose the most productive way to proceed.

Joining the System

In many ways a church is like the human body, "a system which behaves as though it were . . . an organism with a life of its own, with its own internal interconnectedness, multiple contexts, structures and stories," Sawyer maintains. Careful reflection on Paul's metaphor in 1 Corinthians 12:12–31 will do much to help the interim pastor and the congregation move through the interim experience. It is a useful image for understanding congregations and other human systems. Interconnection is the theme in that passage. "As it is, there are many members, yet one body. The eye cannot say to the hand, 'I have no need of you,' nor again the head to the feet, 'I have no need of you.' On the contrary, the members of the body that seem to be weaker are indispensable" (1 Cor. 12:20–22).

Before accepting a call to serve a particular church, the interim pastor should make an initial study of its organization and its system. "Effective interim pastors will then find ways to make quick and significant connections with members of the organization," Sawyer notes. The way these contacts are made will determine the depth and extent of the interim's relationships. It may be useful at this point for the interim to review the first two stages (pre-entry and entry) of an interim pastorate described at the beginning of chapter 4.

How much interim pastors will adapt to the local customs and traditions of the congregation and the community will be a matter for them to decide. Certainly they should become familiar with traditions and expectations, accommodating them as necessary. Ideally, the interim will look for a seasoned elder or church member who can give guidance in these matters. Sawyer suggests, "If members refer to each other by first names or formal titles . . . the interim could follow suit. If pastors are customarily present for prayer breakfasts or quilting circles, [the interim will] find ways and times to attend. . . . The interim leader does not hide his or her own uniqueness or preferences in these matters, but finds a way to be included in the togetherness bonds of the organization."

A word of caution is needed. Objectivity is one of the more important gifts the skilled interim pastor brings to the congregation. If the interim is too emotionally involved in the system or becomes too enmeshed in the process, objectivity may be lost. It is important to maintain a certain detachment along with the sense of belonging. Sawyer notes, "A sense that the interim is simultaneously an insider and an outsider increases the power of the interim to be of service to the organization."

Analyzing the Organization as a System

Rabbi Edwin Friedman, in his landmark book *Generation to Generation: Family Process in Church and Synagogue*, asserts that one may view the congregation as a family, comparing the emotional processes at work in individual families to those in the church. His analysis of the interaction between family systems and work systems offers a model for analyzing each congregation, a model interim pastors will find valuable.

Another equally useful book, which deals more directly with systems theory as it applies to churches, is *Multiple Staff Ministries* by Kenneth R. Mitchell. Two chapters will be especially useful to interim pastors serving in any size church: chapter 2, "Learning a New Way of Thinking," and chapter 3, "Roles, Rules, and Rituals." "Systems behave as though they were persons with lives of their own," Mitchell states. He adds the following principles:

1. Systems regularly act to preserve themselves and to resist change.
2. Systems maintain both external and internal boundaries.
3. Systems are always internally interconnected.
4. Systems assign specialized roles to their members.
5. Systems develop rules and rituals in order to bond members to one another and thus to maintain and preserve the group.

Understanding the meaning of these general criteria of systems thinking will significantly facilitate the analysis of a congregation. Additional resources on church systems are listed in the bibliography.

Analysis begins in the pre-entry stage of an interim call and continues at various levels of intensity throughout the term of service. Initially, analysis is based on what might be called secondary sources: documents that include reports from members of the committee on ministry (COM), the staff of the presbytery, or representatives from the session.

Once the interim pastor is in place, analysis becomes more intense. There are now primary sources of data immediately at hand: church officers, members, staff, and church records. The interim has the opportunity to attend key meetings of church groups as both a leader and an observer. The effective interim will make careful use of all these resources and opportunities to gather information about this congregation and its system.

This analysis should include two elements: the organization and the system. *Organization* here refers to the structure of the congregation and its various parts, such as boards, fellowship groups, couples' clubs, choir, and church school. *System* describes the way those parts work together, work against one another, or just tolerate one another. A congregation may have relatively strong organizations and still function ineffectively as a system. Understanding how the system works can greatly increase the effectiveness of the interim pastor. A file recording how the congregation functions as a system will be a valuable resource throughout the interim period, enabling the interim pastor, the professional staff, and the session to work together more productively.

The following situations are important to recognize during this analysis, and there are sure to be other critical issues and signs to be observed, recorded, and pondered.

> Possible anxiety among the members and officers, its sources and degree of severity
> The level of dependence or independence in relationships with previous pastors and the interim pastor
> The strengths and weaknesses of lay leadership
> The spiritual and emotional condition of the congregation (depression, hope, or indifference)
> The presence or absence of conflict and how it is handled

While it may be relatively easy to observe and record the obvious patterns of the organization, these may be only the first layer of reality. There are probably additional factors that define and govern relationships in the church. As Sawyer points out, "This is analogous to pastoral counseling in which the 'presenting problem' usually leads to more hidden and sometimes more difficult issues in the person's life." Deeper levels of organizational reality might include the following:

> Unresolved issues over relationships with the former pastor
> Entrenched lay leaders who refuse to share or surrender their power
> The extent to which informal lines of authority, boundaries, and rules are in line with the formal constitutional patterns

> The existence of secrets in past or present church
> life and their relative emotional power

Early in the interim period, the interim pastor might form a hypothesis about the system at work in the congregation. As months pass, he or she will get more information which will confirm or deny the hypothesis. This updated assessment will then become the basis for choice of focus and responsibility, the fourth process task.

Connecting with the Denomination

For a Presbyterian church and its pastor, the denomination is an essential part of the system. Sawyer calls it a "super-system." The interim pastor's understanding of the congregation's system is not adequate until that congregation's relationship to the presbytery is clearly understood. Therefore, it will be helpful to review what is written in chapter 5 about the congregation's fourth task: renewing denominational linkages.

Ideally, the interim pastor will join the presbytery in which he or she is in interim service. This act models for the congregation the kind of healthy and supportive regard every member and leader should have toward the presbytery. Furthermore, the interim should attend presbytery meetings often and offer to serve on at least one committee or task force. This will be appreciated in most presbyteries and will assist the interim in joining "the system." Generally, however, interim pastors are not invited to serve on presbytery committees unless they have been members of (and residents in) that presbytery for two or more years.

The interim pastor should be in regular contact with the presbytery executive and the COM, sending progress reports on the congregation's journey through the interim period to the appropriate person or committee at agreed-upon intervals, perhaps quarterly. There may also be personal reports to the COM about the interim's own journey with the congregation.

Should difficulties arise, the wise interim will share information with key leaders in the presbytery and may turn to them for guidance and support. Such sharing and support will come most naturally if mutually respectful ties have already been established. The presbytery's leaders, both professional and voluntary, can be helpful in maintaining the detachment that is necessary and in finding the resources required for effective interim ministry.

The relationship between the interim pastor and the pastor nominating committee is frequently one of the most sensitive areas of work. The advice of the COM should be followed carefully; see the comments in chapter 9.

Focusing and Assuming Responsibility

The two process tasks just discussed provide a major part of the data on which the interim pastor will decide where to focus and how much responsibility to assume in this interim. All interims will remember their individual accountability to God, to the presbytery, and to the session as they focus and select various issues and activities to be the main emphasis of the work during the interim. This is also the time to define clear personal goals and values.

The selection of one or more emphases for major attention may be based on several of the following factors:

> The interim's particular experience and skills
> The interim's understanding and evaluation of the data gathered
> The interim's understanding of what are appropriate roles and responsibilities in this situation, both for the interim and for others in the system
> The degree of openness in the system to each of the issues or activities that the interim has identified as worthy of attention
> The ability of the interim to get the agreement and support of other responsible leaders in the congregation, the presbytery, and other parts of the system
> The interim's own understanding of where God is leading in this particular situation

Some of the more common issues and needs the interim will discover will probably include the following:

> Clarifying leadership roles and structures
> Empowering lay leaders

Furthering spiritual renewal
Improving administrative practices
Promoting healing from grief
Reconciling after conflict

As has already been noted, most congregations are not familiar with the five developmental tasks and will need considerable coaching and guidance. That coaching is part of the fourth process task. It is the interim pastor's responsibility to make sure the congregation understands and is guided appropriately in its work on these tasks.

Exiting and Evaluating

A well-planned and effectively completed farewell is often the best gift that an interim pastor can offer. For the congregation, a healthy exit is a major step toward completion of the fifth developmental task, commitment to a new pastor and a new future. The interim needs to get out of the way in a manner that leaves the congregation feeling comfortable and grateful and ready for the new installed pastor. Certain parts of this task belong exclusively to the interim pastor; others are the responsibility of the congregation.

At the exit stage there will be leaders in the congregation who have come to appreciate the differences in the roles of the lay leaders and the interim pastor. Some members will easily understand what parts of these exiting tasks are theirs and will volunteer to help. As in earlier stages, the perceptive interim will not cripple lay leaders by taking over their jobs. If the exiting and evaluation are to be done well, the interim pastor, the members, and the officers should all assume their own share of these tasks.

The five categories of exiting that belong solely to the interim are (1) the interim's person-to-person relationships, (2) the interim's relationships to the whole "system" that is this church family, (3) contract termination, (4) evaluation, and (5) making a clean break.

The interim pastor's *person-to-person relationships* will include church staff members, church officers and leaders, and probably some individuals who have become especially close because of illnesses, weddings, funerals, or counseling. There will also be people in the presbytery and in the community whose friendship calls for more than perfunctory farewells. In a large congregation, or after a lengthy interim, these person-to-person farewells must necessarily be limited, but some one-to-one good-byes are natural and essential.

Relations with the whole structure—membership, boards, and organizations—also call for appropriate farewells. Some of this will be done at final meetings with each group. Some will be by means of well-planned ceremonies and liturgies in worship services and other gatherings. The best farewells are often planned by the congregation's worship committee and/or the interim pastor. For those who want ideas to prime the pump, there is a model of such a farewell in Appendix H.

Contract termination is initially a part of the original contract negotiation. If clear terms have been written into the interim's contract with the session, all parties will now honor their agreements. If unforeseen difficulties arise, integrity, grace, and justice for everyone should be the goal. Because the presbytery is, through the COM, a party to all interim contracts, the interim pastor will want to inform the presbytery if difficulties have arisen and may rightfully expect presbytery's supportive guidance.

Evaluation, which is discussed in a number of places in this manual, is an important part of the interim experience. Both pastor and congregation will benefit from a thorough, insightful evaluation of the work just completed. The goals are for the interim to glean as much information as possible about the effectiveness of his or her work and for the church and its leaders to have an opportunity to reflect on their own life and ministry. The bibliography and appendixes will suggest a number of useful tools. For the interim the goal is to glean as much constructive information as possible about the effectiveness of his or her work. Another goal is to provide the church and its leaders an opportunity to reflect on their own life and ministry. Again, the bibliography and the appendixes included in this manual will suggest a number of useful tools for evaluation.

Making a clean break in relationships after the exit is completed is as important as making a productive, effective entry. Of course, all pastoral and leadership relationships will be ended, but social relationships must also be concluded in order to allow the new installed pastor to join the system effectively. The easiest way to make a clean break is to take another interim call in a different presbytery. Otherwise some of the church members may think,

That pastor has nothing to do now; why not phone or write or see him or her? This is especially a problem if the former interim is living within the bounds of the presbytery just served. Many interims have said that the most difficult part of the whole experience is to keep a healthy distance from former congregations, both the individual members and their new pastors.

Concluding Reflections on the Five Process Tasks

The health, well-being, effectiveness, and productivity of the interim pastor depend to a large degree on that pastor's understanding of his or her unique role. It also depends on understanding the nature of the tasks that are uniquely his or her responsibility. Sawyer points out that, while the five process tasks correspond in some ways with the congregation's developmental tasks, they must be kept clearly separate in the interim's mind. They are therefore "better suited to personal prayer and journaling, or to discussion with colleagues beyond the church structure, than with the members of the system in transition." Sawyer adds that from time to time "the analysis of the system needs to be reexamined and the hypotheses updated or radically changed." If changes are indicated, they may require refocusing and realignment of responsibilities. Flexibility is an essential quality of every effective interim pastor.

Process in human systems is circular. Sawyer concludes, "Three elements interact: the work of the interim leader, the unfolding of the life of the church organization, and the loving providence of God." With that belief, the interim pastor can confidently join a system and assess it, assume a limited area of focus, do his or her own share of the work, and prepare to leave, confident that no good work is lost in the realm of God.

7

Basic Strategies for Interim Ministry

The work of the interim pastor and of the session during an interim period will be greatly aided by a common understanding as to the type of interim ministry needed in the congregation and an agreement as to the general strategy to be followed in the work of that ministry. At this stage the interim is beginning the task of focusing and assuming responsibility while the session is at work on two of its tasks: coming to terms with their congregation's history and discovering a new identity. Both the interim and the session will be able to work more wisely if they consider which of the basic strategies described in this chapter best fit their circumstances. Conversations about these questions will prove enlightening and productive for all: the interim pastor, the session, and the committee on ministry (COM).

Among the several types of interim ministry, those most commonly found are (1) the maintaining ministry, (2) the changing ministry (principally grief resolution and conflict management), and (3) the developing ministry (usually mission or program development or redevelopment). A particular church may have needs that fit more than one of these types. The goal in congregational analysis is to determine which type of ministry is or should be predominant and which subordinate during the interim.

Rarely is there a time when the circumstances of a congregation exclusively require either a maintaining or a changing interim ministry. Interim pastors, sessions, committees on ministry, and presbyteries need to understand what makes for a healthy relationship between maintenance and change. Every church system tends to organize itself to hold together its community life in a maintenance stance. Every church also has tendencies that will change its life. A schematic way of thinking about a continuum of maintenance and change can help set these different roles in context. In the following diagram, based on a model used by the Alban Institute, the diagonal separating the two tendencies represents the many points from which the pastoral tasks of the congregation can be approached.

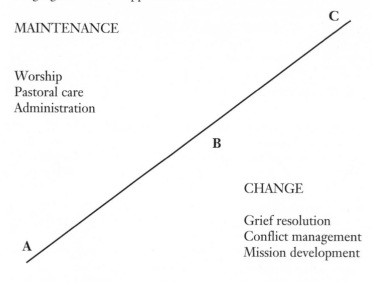

MAINTENANCE

Worship
Pastoral care
Administration

B

CHANGE

Grief resolution
Conflict management
Mission development

A

C

Point *A* is the characteristic stance of that interim pastor whose role is thought of entirely as maintenance. Point *C*, the opposite extreme, represents the role of the interim pastor (or consultant) who, having little commitment to maintenance functions, makes interventions calculated to assist the organization to make changes in its life. Most interim pastors would operate somewhere between these extremes, probably working closer to Point *A*, depending on their skills, interests, and understanding of their role and the needs of the situation. The installed pastor would ordinarily operate at some hypothetical Point *B*, toward the center of the diagonal.

The concerns for maintenance and for change are both appropriate. The style and skill of the interim pastor and the needs of the particular situation dictate the mix of maintenance and change that is wise for a specific pastorate. Many believe there is a place for the interim whose focus is purely on maintenance, just as there is a place for the one whose primary responsibility is to be a catalyst for change. Some knowledgeable interims assert, however, that because seeking a pastor is itself a new and change-making experience for a congregation, there is never a congregation that requires only maintenance services.

If there are diverse needs in a large congregation, the various tasks may be carried out best by a team of interim pastors. This has worked well in a number of places. It is the responsibility of the session in consultation with the COM to determine what is needed in each case and to prepare an appropriate position description. It is possible that the interim may want to negotiate changes in the position description during the pre-entry or entry stages of the work, though that may be difficult to do once a covenant or contract has been signed.

The Maintaining Ministry

The maintaining ministry may be described as the continuing of helpful, supportive, strong programs and services through which a congregation's basic life is nourished, the pastoral tasks are done, the educational and fellowship programs sustained, and the administrative life carried on, to be turned over largely unchanged to the new pastor. Such an interim strategy is appropriate for many congregations. Even when a church is diagnosed as "sick" by its own session, interim pastor, or presbytery leaders, major surgery may be unnecessary if a change of diet and the right kind of exercise will do the job.

The interim pastor is often expected to be the principal preaching minister, the administrator, and the head of staff (paid and/or volunteer) and to share in some of the pastoral calling and counseling. The interim is nearly always the moderator of the session and should be welcome in meetings of the trustees and deacons. In a multiple staff situation, other pastors may take turns attending these meetings. The interim can also be helpful by being available for meetings of other groups, such as young people, older adults, and singles. He or she is expected to take the lead in celebrating the sacraments and ordinances of the church but should be willing to share that responsibility with other ordained members of the staff, if any.

It is usually the interim pastor's task to provide continuity, for congregations are sensitive to sudden change. During an interim, some members of the congregation will imagine changes in worship forms, even though the pastor is trying to follow well-established routines. The simple fact that there is now a different pastor conducting worship and preaching may give the impression that there have been wider changes.

The real problem, however, may not be so subtle. There may be individuals, groups, or official bodies within the church who are eager for certain changes, and some may be long overdue. Even in a church needing a maintaining ministry, the interim pastor is wise to consider any proposed changes carefully with the session.

Guiding Change in a Maintaining Ministry

The Rev. Terry Foland, an experienced trainer of interim pastors with the Disciples of Christ and the Interim Ministry Network, has made a list of important considerations to review before changes are made during an interim period. His list, with some revisions, follows:

1. Whose agenda is it? Whose need is being met? Be sure any new programs are really wanted by the congregation. Pet programs of the interim pastor should not be forced on the church.

2. Collaborate with the session in planning. Use appropriate structures to bring about change. The interim period may be a good time to tackle major stumbling blocks and difficult problems such as organizational structure, bylaws, church staff, or services and programs, any of which may be a source of conflict.

3. Make changes slowly.

4. Add on rather than eliminate, if possible. Offer choices between the new and the old.

5. Carefully assess the possible effects of the change. Who will gain? Who will lose? What is to be gained? What must be given up?

6. Prepare people for the change. Give them a chance to talk about it.

7. Present changes as provisional or experimental.

8. Do not create changes that will be a problem for the new pastor. Patterns of the interim pastor's personal and professional behavior may be difficult to match; for example, intense pastoral calling or counseling, doing the work of the church secretary, the deacons, or the sexton.

9. Develop criteria and make time for an evaluation of any actual changes. This sets a useful pattern for the future.

Sermons for the Maintaining Ministry

An experienced interim pastor, speaking at a Ghost Ranch seminar, made the following observations about worship and preaching in the interim setting:

> The single most effective opportunity shared with a congregation is worship. All parts of the service may be properly utilized to provide transitional emphasis and impetus. Worship is both a sacred event and a sacred experience. It is perhaps the one area of congregational life least amenable to change. Worship is a shared link with the past, present, and future of each person's faith. It is affirmation, confirmation, and declaration. This is a time when sense and feeling are openly responsive. Each person brings a set of expectations to worship. Once these expectations are met, members of the congregation will be open and receptive to other possibilities.

Preaching is only one part of worship, but within Presbyterian tradition it is an integral part. No one should try interim work who isn't reasonably good at sermon preparation and delivery. Effective ministry depends on new and fresh sermons related to these people and their situation. An interim pastorate is neither the time nor the place, if indeed there ever *is* a place, for a cassette-service diet of other preachers' sermons. The congregation faces special needs and concerns, disappointment, or open hostility, having lost a beloved leader, whether by death, relocation, or retirement. Problems regularly resident in any congregation are intensified in the interim period. An interim pastor may draw on a personal sermonic file, but every sermon should be sharpened to meet specific local needs.

While every sermon needs to be tailored to the individual congregation, there are a number of biblical themes and texts that a preacher might develop to deal with a congregation's need to understand what is happening in the interim experience.

Celebrating Our History

> Exodus 3:1–6, 9–12
> Deuteronomy 32:1–3, 7–12a
> Luke 24:13–31a

Waiting with Patience and Hope

> Psalms 27; 103:1–13
> Romans 8:14–25

Rediscovering the Church

> Genesis 28:10–22
> Matthew 28:16–20
> Ephesians 2:13–22

Our Presbyterian Heritage

> Elders and the Law
>> Deuteronomy 27:1–10
> Elders Noted in the New Testament
>> Acts 14:21–23
>> 1 Timothy 5:17–19
>> Titus 1:5–9
>> James 5:13–16
> Understanding the Uses of Power
>> Job 38 and 39, selected verses
>> Mark 4:35–41

One advantage of staying in fellowship with other interim pastors is the stimulus that close communication offers, not only in sharing themes for preaching but in exchanging ideas in many other areas of common concern.

More Aspects of the Maintaining Ministry

Keeping a congregation informed during the interim interval is basic. Communication can take many different forms to maintain interest, participation, and support. Regular and adequate provision of information concerning session actions, programs and events of the church, and the work of the pastor nominating committee (PNC) builds trust and develops confidence in the future.

Leadership training events are natural ways to maintain and

strengthen the congregation's structure. There is usually a need for church-officer training classes because many officers are not sure of their roles. The interim pastor need not always be personally responsible for conducting such training but should see that it is done—and done well.

The Changing Ministry

Many congregations facing a period between installed pastors will need an interim pastor with specialized skills to handle various, sometimes complex, issues that clearly require change. If there is a need to clear up deep hurts from previous church conflicts or heal long-standing feuds, a special kind of grief resolution may be required. Any sort of crisis, such as the public disgrace of the previous pastor or a congregational split, will call for a change-oriented interim ministry with a focus on conflict or grief resolution. Environmental or economic factors may determine the principal strategy needed in an interim pastorate. When a change occurs in the character of the church's neighborhood, when a significant mission development opportunity appears, when a congregation is facing questions about whether or not it ought to be dissolved, change possibilities must be considered.

Among the several kinds of changes that may be called for during the interim period, three will be examined here: grief resolution, conflict management, and reconciliation. Any of them may require crisis intervention in extreme circumstances.

Grief Resolution

Often a congregation that has just lost its pastor goes through stages of grief similar to those described by John Bowlby: (1) sadness and anger, (2) disorganization and depression, and (3) reorganization. Obviously there are differences in these stages when a congregation wants a pastor to leave, but there will still be some grief and guilt that will need the interim pastor's careful attention.

When a longtime pastor leaves the congregation, the need for grief work is obvious. It is essential for the interim pastor to be fully conscious of this dynamic and to discuss it with the session. Pastor and session can then plan together to work through the various stages of grief in the life of the session and of the congregation.

The temptation for the interim pastor is to build trust on a personal basis. This move is ill-advised; it leaves the congregation doubly bereft when the interim goes. Interim pastors have an opportunity to use their own dependability, integrity, and professional skills to help a congregation to let go of its past—and of the interim pastor as well. The interim pastor is placed at a unique point for helping the congregation discover itself and work on key dynamics of its life. Ordinary events of a congregation's life can be used to assist growth beyond loss, grief, and disorganization. A number of resources available to help pastors understand and deal with personal and community grief are listed in the bibliography.

Consider the following strategies and techniques in working with grief:

1. State (in talks, sermons, informal meetings, and personal conversation) and act out a basic acceptance that the past is gone and the future is not yet, and that is OK for now. A sermon series helping the congregation to recall, understand, and celebrate its own history can be useful. Allowing church members to verbalize recollections of the past can help them deal directly and positively with grief and guilt. Such a program should not be attempted, however, until it has been considered by the session.

2. Be open to renegotiate details of the task so that energy gets shifted to where the real congregational hurts are.

3. Reinterpret various seasons, such as spring and fall, Lent and Advent, to include the life/death dynamic.

4. Deal realistically with the congregation's experiences of life/death/resurrection as they occur liturgically, during pastoral visits, and at memorial services, funerals, births, baptisms, and weddings.

5. Make it clear that the interim pastor is truly leaving when the contract is over and is not available to become the congregation's pastor.

Conflict Management

Churches in serious conflict or churches with major problems of other kinds such as a previous pastor's grave misconduct, whether sexual or financial, are among those which have most appreciated the services of a qualified interim pastor. Persons who understand conflict management and are skilled in handling it can often make the difference between a relatively brief period of conflict resolution (and growth-oriented change) and a long, sometimes painful avoidance of issues and problems or a fumbling attempt to resolve critical difficulties.

Generally, the course of least resistance is to pretend that conflict does not exist, or that the differences are minor and will resolve themselves if everyone is "nice." It all centered in the pastor, some say, and will disappear as soon as the pastor is gone. Such attitudes tend to cover up real disagreements, allowing them to fester until they erupt into major difficulty, usually sometime after a new pastor is called. The wise session or COM will make sure this does not happen.

It may sometimes be necessary to bring hidden conflicts or long-unresolved differences into the open. Occasionally one must exacerbate or stimulate a conflict in order that problems can be identified and dealt with adequately. It would be wise for the interim to be in close consultation with the COM, the presbytery executive, and/or members of the session before taking such an approach, however.

Finding an interim pastor skilled in conflict management may be the most appropriate answer to these difficulties. This requires careful matching of the interim and the congregation to be served. The experienced COM will take leadership in guiding the session of a troubled church to persuade them that an interim pastorate is a good idea at this time. Finding the right person is imperative. In such cases, both the executive presbyter and the COM will find that thorough knowledge of their own interim pastors will pay real dividends. Churchwide Personnel Services of the National Ministries Division at the General Assembly headquarters is the place to write or phone for personal information forms of interim pastors (see bibliography). The COM must trust the experienced intentional interim pastor, once selected, to guide the session and the congregation in identifying and acknowledging their problems and in working on them. The COM, the presbytery executive, and others in the presbytery who can be helpful will naturally stand with the interim in such a situation, making sure to provide all possible support and encouragement.

At times it may be wise for the session or the COM to consider calling in specialists in conflict management or persons skilled in systems analysis and organizational development. These consultants can function primarily as short-term change agents and problem solvers and guide the interim pastor, the session, and the congregation in responding to special needs. Such a specialist can address some of the things that stimulate conflict, such as inadequate communication, destructive behavior patterns, inadequate attention to process, an organizational pattern unsuited to functions, or lack of appropriate satisfactions and rewards for members.

If systems specialists are to be employed, the interim pastor should share fully in the planning process and welcome and work closely with any consultant who may be brought into the picture. Clear-cut written statements of responsibility and accountability for the consultant specialist and for the interim pastor are essential if this course is followed. A good consultant will insist on such written agreements. If that does not happen, the interim will want to confer with COM representatives or with the session itself to see that contracts and understandings are put in writing and honored. In conflict, strong and thoughtful administrative leadership is essential.

A critical aspect of working with a congregation in conflict is identifying the level of intensity of the conflict at hand. Knowing about these various levels will guide the COM, the interim, and the session in determining what kind of help is needed to manage most conflict situations. A General Assembly Task Force on Pastor/Congregation Conflict named and described five levels of conflict intensity in churches, which point up the complexity of any work in church conflict. Described more fully in Appendix F, they are (1) a problem to solve, (2) a disagreement, (3) a contest, (4) fight or flight, and (5) an intractable situation—"war."

Most trained interim pastors will be equipped to handle conflict at levels 1 and 2. Level 3 requires special training in conflict management, available through the National Ministries Division of the General Assembly; the Alban Institute; the Interim Ministry Network; and other groups specializing in advanced training for pastors and church officers. The COM should strive to have at least some active members who are trained to work with conflict up to and including level 3. The bibliography lists additional useful resources for managing church conflict; the COM and the interim pastor should consider reading and keeping at hand several of those works. The Conflict Task Force recommended that only professional consultants should be employed to deal with conflict in any congregation at levels 4 or 5. The interim ought not to be involved at these levels.

In larger, deeply troubled congregations it may be necessary to bring in a team of interim pastors: a head of staff, an associate pastor, and even special consultants, all of them on interim status or with special contracts. When such an approach has been employed in the past, all parties involved—the session, the congregation, and the interim staff—have responded wholeheartedly to a clearly perceived emergency, and the results generally have been gratifying.

Reconciliation

A congregation involved in significant difficulty will need an interim pastor with ability not only to manage conflict but also to promote reconciliation. Groups within the congregation may be fighting each other. Relationships with the presbytery may need mending. There may also be serious trouble with neighboring churches, organizations, or persons in the community. Objectivity and a warm personal style in working with individuals, as well as with boards and committees, are critical elements in promoting healing. Some knowledge of the dynamics of conflict and of processes that promote understanding and good health in organizations are important too. At best, the interim will also possess skills in mediation or will know where to find consultants with such skills. In these circumstances everything the interim does— such as preaching or leading worship and using small groups for Bible study or other kinds of discussion—will contribute to the healing process if designed to do so.

A few practical suggestions are helpful for the interim pastor who becomes the one to mediate between conflicted parties. Mediation in conflict works best when the mediator is trusted by all parties to the conflict, is not defensive, is deliberate (does not move through the process too fast), is patient (willing to review and repeat any steps when that is useful), is objective (does not make judgments about right or wrong but seeks to bring all concerned parties together to help them reach agreement), and is always present when any of the parties to the conflict talk together about it.

The mediation process generally has three steps: (1) analysis: "What's going on here?" (2) negotiation: "What can be done about it?" and (3) resolution: "How do we settle this?" Moving through this process is not, however, as easy as these three steps may suggest. Interim pastors who consider serving conflicted churches are well advised to seek training in conflict management first.

The Developing Ministry

Most presbyteries today urge or require that a mission study of the church and the community, sometimes called a self-study, be made during the interim period. Such a study may be conducted in a variety of ways: by the session; by a special committee, usually appointed by the session; by the PNC; or in some other way. Often this study is made with the assistance of the COM or a presbytery committee responsible for mission strategy. Such a study generally includes a review of the policies and organization of the congregation. It may also include the development of long-range goals and objectives and the establishment of ongoing processes for evaluation. This study enables the session to know what its goals for ministry and mission ought to be. It enables the PNC to recognize the abilities and experiences needed in the pastor now to be sought. The interim pastor should be aware of the presbytery policy and the persons and instruments used by the presbytery in this study.

The interim may sometimes be asked by the COM to serve as a liaison or resource person in this study. When the session and presbytery agree that special mission development or redevelopment strategies are called for, it may be necessary to redefine the role of the interim pastor as it relates to changes in congregation or session objectives. These are times when the task must include more than simply assuring continuity in the life of the congregation. If particular short-range goals or other changes are needed they should be negotiated by the COM, the session, and perhaps other key leaders of the congregation. Otherwise the interim pastor may set up conditions that will lead to confusion or conflict.

The interim experience can be a time for making significant changes in a congregation's mission direction and total life. Church programs and groups already in existence may be used to prepare for change, or they may be left intact while new programs and new organizations are introduced for the purpose of developing change in the mission, program, and services of the congregation. The presbytery may have special committees to assist in any subsequent development or redevelopment of mission programs the session and the congregation choose to undertake. The interim, session, and presbytery are a team whose objective is to lead the congregation into a new future under a new pastor.

8

The Interim Pastor in a Multiple Staff Church

A popular piece of playground equipment in many communities resembles a giant spiderweb made of ropes. Some webs are designed to resemble a geodesic dome, the center of the web being higher than the perimeter. Children find it a real challenge to climb to the top of the dome. Staying on top is relatively easy until another child decides to play on the web too. The second child sets the entire structure into motion. If other children deliberately shake the web, a lot of waving, bouncing movement is created, making it very difficult for the child at the top to hang on. Even the descent can be tricky.

Kenneth R. Mitchell in his book *Multiple Staff Ministries* notes that the playground spiderweb visually illustrates the significance of connectedness in human systems such as a church staff. Each time a new person enters the web, everyone already on the web is affected. Even minimal disturbances will set the whole web in motion. Everyone on the web will move up and down or side to side in ways they cannot themselves control. Interconnectedness is at the heart of systems theory.

Although this experience can be fun, it may be distressing for those whose position on the web is threatened by a new player. Think now about the arrival of an interim pastor in a multiple staff church. The entire staff is forced to reevaluate itself and its position, individually and as a group. All relationships are changed in one way or another. Anxiety over the future, immediate and long-range, is to be expected. One pastor noted that the level and intensity of staff anxiety increases geometrically with each additional staff person involved. Careful attention to all staff members—professional and support staff, paid and volunteer—is essential if the interim tasks are to be completed. A staff member can either em-

power or sabotage the newcomer. Everyone impacts everyone
else, among staff and in the congregation as a whole. Because interconnectedness of the church staff is more immediate and more
obvious than connections within the congregation, good staff relationships are basic in any interim assignment. In multiple staff
churches, healthy professional relationships are crucial for productive interim ministry.

Only two permanent pastoral offices are recognized in the
Presbyterian Church: pastor and associate pastor (*Book of Order* G-
6.0202). A particular church may elect co-pastors who are equal in
authority, but there is no provision for what has been called "head
of staff" or "senior pastor." Those terms are used only informally,
though widely, within the Presbyterian Church. It is important to
recognize this parity of the ministry in our theology and polity.
Understanding this concept is essential to building a healthy staff
relationship.

Parity in the church, theologically and ecclesiastically, is not
the same as parity of experience, competence, or spiritual gifts.
Pastors who are termed "head of staff" or "senior pastor" are usually given these positions because they have more experience than
others on the staff. In one sense, the church constitution acknowledges these differences when it states that "an associate . . .
pastor shall be directed in his or her work by the pastor in consultation with the session." The *Book of Order* further states, "The official relationship of an associate . . . pastor to a church is not dependent upon that of a pastor" (G-14.0501f). Once an associate
pastor has been installed, that pastor's ecclesiastical standing in
the congregation and in the presbytery is on a par with any other
installed pastor, including one who may be called "head of staff."

Interim pastors, whatever their position on a church staff,
should appreciate the significant differences between service in an
installed position and in an interim position. This chapter will examine these differences and propose ways to accomplish the special tasks of interim ministry, the developmental tasks of the congregation, and the process tasks of the interim pastor.

The Interim Head of Staff

Interim pastors who serve multiple staff churches as interim
head of staff (IHOS) should be familiar with the theory and practice of interim ministry presented earlier in this manual.

What are the differences between an installed and an interim position? Often the IHOS will join pastors who are installed in their positions while the interim is, of course, temporary. These installed pastors may have significant tenure when the IHOS arrives. Their experience can be invaluable in the tasks of entry and joining the system, provided the IHOS uses this resource.

In another church the interim pastor may be joining a clergy staff that includes one or more of other interims. As head of staff, he or she must keep in mind that other pastor colleagues in that church are also joining the system and also have interim tasks to complete, as well as the work included in their individual job descriptions.

The IHOS who is working with an installed associate pastor can be greatly assisted in the process tasks. The interim pastor should be open to receive all the help the associate can offer, and the associate pastor should allow the time and energy required to make sure the IHOS gets a good start. They should agree to spend time with each other in designing a plan to help the IHOS join the system. The associate will have a pastor's view of the congregation and its system and can share insights that church members and officers may not have. The associate can offer information about how he or she worked with the former head of staff and what was helpful in that relationship. The associate will also have experience to share about working with the others on the paid and volunteer staff, as well as suggestions about ways in which he or she is prepared to help.

The IHOS can discuss interim theory with the associate and suggest ways the associate can be of help in each of the process and developmental tasks. The time spent in discussion with the installed associate pastor is a wise investment.

Much has been written about ministry in the multiple staff church. The IHOS is well advised to review some of the literature in this field, especially the book by Kenneth Mitchell just mentioned. What has worked well for an installed head of staff may not be as successful for an interim who does not have the privilege of designing and implementing a long-range plan. Rarely will the IHOS have the privilege of choosing any of the clergy staff. If additional interim pastors are to be employed, a high degree of mutual compatibility is of critical importance. Ideally the IHOS would have significant input in their selection.

A multiple staff ministry that works well, Mitchell observes, tends to have stability over a period of time. But stability is exactly the element usually absent during an interim. There are, however, two other elements that enable a staff to succeed: (1) satisfaction and happiness in their work together and (2) visible results of that work. It may be assumed, then, that the IHOS will be most successful when all possible stability is assured for the ongoing staff and the congregation. It is not usually the role of the IHOS to seek to remove anyone on the church staff unless that person is clearly not functioning effectively during the interim period.

The desired results in multiple staff ministry—satisfaction and happiness and visible results—are most likely to be achieved by a modified team approach in which the head of staff coordinates the work of the team and takes final responsibility. In a sense, everyone on the team is accountable to everyone else. Authority and responsibility are not destroyed; they are simply defined, limited, and shared. Such an arrangement fosters rich communication among all team members, without the IHOS controlling communications. Daily operations are conducted on a peer basis, as the IHOS allows others maximum freedom in their work.

This kind of team approach will enable the IHOS to build trust and gain respect in the congregation as well as among the staff. In doing this the IHOS will function in various roles at different times with members of the church staff, including serving as loyal friend and adviser, teacher, coach, consultant, counselor, and colleague. The anxiety that always accompanies change reaches a high intensity among church staff members during an interim. The senior pastor needs to be particularly sensitive to this factor. Because some of the staff will need frequent reassurance, encouragement, and support, the IHOS will focus on group building and morale building in the first few weeks of the interim. Personal and corporate grief work will be encouraged and supported. To achieve some of these goals, Duncan Cameron, a pastor who has served as IHOS in a number of larger churches, states that in addition to spending significant time and energy directly with the staff, he also makes an effort to compliment and commend the church staff individually and before the congregation, in board meetings, newsletters, and other communications.

Every head of staff, whether installed or interim, will make sure every paid staff member has a clear job description, a written contract with all terms spelled out, and regular performance and compensation reviews. The interim pastor must never assume that these administrative tasks are in place. Rather, he or she will review all the personnel policies, papers, and processes and, if any are inadequate, will work with the session and the personnel committee to establish effective personnel practices. The earlier the analysis of the personnel practices is in effect, the more likely needed improvements can be made. Here the principles for guiding change during an interim time will need to be carefully observed (see chapter 7).

Regular staff meetings will provide opportunity for the IHOS to be listener, teacher, coach, and administrator. There will also be individual meetings with staff members, as often as needed. Whether meeting with the entire staff or individually, the IHOS will seek to remain a calming presence, listening to concerns, offering reassurance, or providing guidance.

Duncan Cameron suggests that another important task of the IHOS is "running interference for the staff." He says, "If someone is making inappropriate demands on them, I encourage the staff to refer the person to me. . . . The staff need to know they can count on the support of the head of staff."

Above all, staff members need to be reminded of the importance of their own self-care, taking regular days off, getting away from the demands of work and the congregation. Vacation time and regular study leaves should not be interfered with. The responsible IHOS will not only support reasonable self-care for colleagues and associates but will set an example of such behavior.

The Interim Co-Pastor

Though initially only the interim pastors were solo pastors or heads of staff, the success of this form of ministry has led the Presbyterian Church to expand the *Book of Order* to provide for interim co-pastors (ICPs) and interim associate pastors (IAPs). Experience has verified the benefits of using an interim when any vacancy develops in a ministerial staff.

Calling an ICP or IAP provides professional leadership promptly when it is needed. It also offers the session and the installed pastors an opportunity to review the roles and relationships in the church and to reflect on new ways of working without making long-term personnel commitments before the congregation is ready.

The ICP and the IAP need to be well acquainted with basic interim theory and practice as outlined in earlier chapters of this manual. However, there are some differences in the way these theories and practices are applied when the interim is serving on a church staff.

The roles of co-pastor and interim co-pastor are stated in the *Book of Order* (G-14.0501c and G-14.0513b). Upon the departure of an installed co-pastor, if the congregation and session (in consultation with the committee on ministry [COM]) decide to call another, it is wise to fill the position temporarily by calling an ICP.

An intentional and trained ICP will often understand the dynamics of interim situations better than the installed co-pastor and can therefore guide in the needed grief work and other interim tasks. In addition, the ICP will know the five developmental tasks of the congregation (see chapter 5) and can assist the session and other church members in working through them, as well as assuring that the installed co-pastor is not burned out by trying to carry the workload of two persons.

If no one replaces the former co-pastor, the session and the congregation may get used to the idea that they do not need co-pastors and can get along with a smaller or less experienced staff. Trying to economize on staff and salaries during an interim time often diminishes the congregation's self-image and enthusiasm for its mission and ministry. It can be a real mistake.

The importance of true compatibility between the two co-pastors, whether installed or interim, deserves careful thought. The two personalities must be able to work well together, have a common vision of the church, and hold mutually compatible theological positions. Ideally, they will have interests and skills that are complementary rather than overlapping. Each must have true flexibility, humility, and patience. It is not easy to be a co-pastor, whether installed or interim.

The Interim Associate Pastor

If the session desires, they may choose to call an IAP instead of an ICP, a decision that should be made in consultation with the COM or its representative. The role of an IAP is stated in the *Book of Order* (G-14.0513c). He or she is invited to maintain the level of programs and services the church has provided while the search for a new associate is under way. The IAP will also offer guidance in work on the five developmental tasks to those groups he or she serves in the congregation. The whole congregation will need to grieve to some degree when an associate pastor leaves. Those groups with which the associate worked most closely—youth, church school teachers, deacons, or others—will especially need to work through their feelings.

The session may also use this opportunity to experiment with a different range of programs and services, a new job description for the IAP, or new staff relationships and accountabilities.

Occasionally a session will attempt to save money by not hiring an IAP. This false economy will result in a step backward in the life of the church. If youth ministry has been part of the associate's job, it is important to remember that one year in the life of a teenager can seem like five years in the life of an adult. If a program is diminished or dropped for a year or longer, some young people will leave the church, perhaps never to return. There may be a drop in church income as well, if some members reason that, because no one is doing the job, the church doesn't need as much money.

While lay leaders in the congregation may be able to take over many of the tasks of an associate pastor who has departed, only an ordained pastor can celebrate the sacraments and ordinances of the church. When a session considers not calling an IAP, one question to address is whether the pastor who remains as head of staff can carry the additional pastoral responsibilities without suffering overload and burnout. Even the most gifted youth advisers, church educators, deacons, and trustees are rarely able to carry out the pastoral care, counseling, and related services usually provided by an associate pastor.

The Five
Developmental Tasks

In a multiple staff situation, the interim pastor, whether head of staff, co-pastor, or associate pastor, is responsible for informing the others on the church staff about the five developmental tasks and their significance. The staff should then determine together how they will acquaint the congregation with these tasks and which pastor will be the coach or guide for each one. Chapter 5 offers ideas for developing a plan to implement the congregation's work.

When serving with an installed head of staff, the IAP will find that some interim tasks are easier to accomplish while others are more difficult because they are less clearly defined or perceived. Most commonly, the IAP will find that the transition the congregation is experiencing is minimal for those who had little contact with the former associate pastor, while for others the associate's departure is a major loss. (It is rare that two or more pastors leave a congregation at the same time.)

One of the first concerns is whether or not the key leaders of the congregation (the head of staff, the session, and the personnel committee) understand the dynamics of interim ministry. If not, how can the IAP acquaint them with those dynamics? They need to know at least enough to allow him or her time to work on the special interim tasks as well as the ongoing church program. Time for this work ought to be part of the contract negotiations in the pre-entry and entry stages of the interim. In some presbyteries the COM requires that the five developmental tasks be listed in all interim job descriptions. Thus everyone involved acknowledges that these tasks are a legitimate part of the interim's work. The head of staff who appreciates the validity of these tasks may even assist with some of them. The IAP will welcome such support.

Because one of the responsibilities sometimes given to an IAP is an examination of denominational connections, questions that may be raised could include the following: What curriculum or program materials does this church have? Are there denominational resources that might be used? Do the youth programs tie in with presbytery, synod, or General Assembly activities? The interim period is the logical time to review such policies and practices, and the IAP is the person who can encourage key congregational leaders to consider their denominational connections. All such activity, however, should be undertaken with the full knowledge and prior approval of the head of staff, the session, and/or session committees.

In addressing the fifth developmental task, commitment to new leadership, the IAP can make a major contribution to a smooth, happy, and wholesome transition to the next associate pastor. Suggestions in chapter 5 can be adapted to the circumstances of his or her departure and the arrival of the new installed associate pastor. Though this is the task of the congregation or special groups within it, the IAP can be the guide.

The Five
Process Tasks

Almost everything in chapter 6 on the process tasks of the interim pastor applies, with adaptations, to the IAP. A major distinction will be the fact that the IAP is usually accountable first to the head of staff and then to the session or its personnel committee. In some cases the IAP will also be accountable to other individuals or committees in the congregation. Like all Presbyterian ministers, the IAP also has accountability to the presbytery, to the COM, and to God. It is with these accountabilities in mind that the IAP addresses the process tasks: joining the system, analyzing the organization as a system, connecting with the denomination, focusing and assuming responsibility, and exiting and evaluating.

The IAP will establish a cordial working relationship with the head of staff and all others who have any oversight of his or her work and can look to these "overseers" for guidance and support. The head of staff (or key leaders in areas of the IAP's work) will guide the IAP in joining the system as well as in analyzing the organization as a system. Because these leaders are themselves part of this organization and system, the IAP should keep in mind that their objectivity may be limited and will want to consider privately just how he or she perceives their places in that system. COM or presbytery staff may be of real assistance here by sharing an objective view of the congregation and its staff and lay leaders. It is important, however, for an IAP always to keep in mind the distinctions between being a co-pastor and an associate pastor. One of the most serious mistakes an associate pastor (installed or interim) can make is to assume and to behave as though he or she is co-pastor with the head of staff.

The IAP's connection with the denomination is as important as the interim pastor's. Suggestions in chapter 6 on this point should be reviewed by the IAP and discussed with the head of staff. The IAP's relationship to the presbytery and the denomination will be a model for the youth of the congregation, as well as for those adults with whom the IAP works directly. If the IAP and the head of staff disagree on this, they should work out their differences during pre-entry negotiations. The COM or its representative should approve all agreements and can mediate differences, if necessary.

When the time comes for exit and evaluation, the IAP should recognize that these are both individual processes and group processes. The IAP has personal responsibilities in exiting and should make his or her own evaluation of the entire interim experience. These tasks, however, also involve members and groups in the congregation, and the IAP should be ready to guide them as the interim draws to a close.

If both the head of staff and the associate are serving as interim pastors in the same church, the dynamics of the system change significantly for everyone. Each interim on such a team has contributions to make to the session, to the congregation, to one another, and to the whole system. They will need to be in close and frequent consultation with each other and with others in the system if the experience is to be healthy for everyone.

Usually the IHOS will be called to the church first and will immediately begin work on the five process tasks. When the IAP arrives, work on the process tasks continue for both pastors. This may be carried on jointly and individually. Both pastors must keep in mind that they are in an interim relationship with the church and with each other.

Often the IHOS will leave before the IAP leaves. When that is clear, plans can be made with that timing in mind. Joint planning for any departure will assure mutuality in the working relationship. The goal is to complete all the interim tasks, the congregation's developmental tasks, and the pastors' process tasks before either pastor leaves. These statements assume the ideal, however, which may not be fully realized. The congregation's tasks and the interim pastors' tasks may not be neatly finished on any particular schedule. Close and frequent consultation and real flexibility are essential.

When the IHOS and the IAP are trained, intentional interims, both will understand the congregation's tasks and their own tasks so that they can cooperate fully in coaching the congregation, either sharing that work or dividing it task by task. If an IAP is working with an IHOS who is unfamiliar with interim theory and practice, the associate should seek counsel of the COM for ideas on how best to deal with this situation. Conversation with other interim pastors serving in that presbytery or in nearby presbyteries may also be useful. The IAP should be careful before simply suggesting that the IHOS read a book about interim ministry, even this manual, or that the IHOS should take interim training. Such advice should come from the COM or from the presbytery executive.

Finding the Next Call

After the term of service is completed, it is as important for the IAP in a multiple staff church to make a clean break from the congregation as it is for any other interim pastor. The best way to make that break is to find another job, preferably at some distance. The suggestions made in this manual for the pastor seeking an interim opportunity apply to the IAP as well. The recommendation of the head of staff will be invaluable, whether the IAP is seeking another interim pastorate or an installed position. Even if the IAP chooses not to use the head as a reference on the personal information form (PIF), potential "employers" will still want to talk with the head of staff regarding the IAP's work.

Flexibility, a key quality for any successful interim pastor, applies to the search process as much as to any other part of the work. Does this mean a given interim should be open to service as a solo pastor, an associate pastor, or as head of staff? A careful answer is, "Yes and no!" The answer is yes only if the person has the experience, training, and professional and personal gifts to do well in any of those jobs. The answer is no for most pastors, because few are truly prepared to do all those jobs, and those who say they can will give the impression that they are not focused and that they do not know which of their skills are strongest. Such indiscriminate job seeking raises questions about the pastor's self-understanding and good judgment.

The wise interim will consult the Call Referral Services staff at the General Assembly headquarters regarding how to prepare the most useful PIF and how best to use the resources of the placement system.

Interim pastors have served well in a great variety of Presbyterian churches and in a wide range of interim positions. One large congregation engaged four interim pastors at one time! Many small churches have had half-time "tentmaker" or interim pastors. There is a long list of variations on these patterns of service. Congregations and presbyteries alike have recognized the value of this form of ministry, which is clearly focused and adapted to the needs of the church when a search for a new pastor is under way. That is the reason the interim pastor categories in the *Book of Order* have been expanded by adding ICP and IAP. Congregations with a multiple staff ministry are beginning to discover how greatly enriched their churches can be when they fill ministerial staff vacancies with trained, intentional interim pastors.

9

Key Relationships for the Interim Pastor

Interim ministries can have many uncertainties. For pastors who move frequently, there is almost never an opportunity to develop long-term or close friends in any congregation or community. Loneliness and personal disorientation may be frequent problems. Because familiar faces and scenes are generally far removed, these pastors will be greatly benefited by a close relationship to a good support group. Similarly, interims who are settled in a home of their own but are commuting some distance to the church they serve, or who serve a nearby church, will also profit from additional fellowship and nourishment. A support group can satisfy both personal and professional needs. If one does not exist in a particular presbytery, the interim will be well rewarded by organizing some support program, either among Presbyterian interims or ecumenically.

Where there are only a few Presbyterian interim pastors in a given presbytery, it may be possible either to establish a group or to join an already established ecumenical group in the area. Interim pastors are growing more popular in a number of denominations with call systems, as well as in some with appointment systems. The Interim Ministry Network (IMN) office can provide names and addresses of network members living in a particular region. The Association of Presbyterian Interim Ministry Specialists (APIMS) may also be able to assist interims wishing to form support groups. Addresses for IMN and APIMS are listed in the bibliography.

In addition to finding or creating a local group of persons with enough common experiences and interests to provide satisfying and nourishing exchanges on a regular basis, the interim pastor will also benefit from a wider network of supportive persons and groups.

Both the presbytery and the session should plan personal support for both the interim pastor and the pastor's spouse, if there is one. Such support should respond to spiritual, emotional, psychological, and other personal needs. There may be persons or groups in the congregation, the community, or the presbytery who can provide part of the kind of support that is needed. If not, the committee on ministry (COM), or perhaps a presbytery committee on nurture or leadership development, could carry this responsibility.

Beyond the presbytery, the interim may seek supportive connections in higher governing bodies and elsewhere. The suggestions that follow apply both to small groups and to larger networks, which an individual interim may want to build. Connections established beyond the presbytery are ones that can remain in place and continue to be productive for the interim pastor almost anywhere he or she may be called to serve. Such a larger extended network for support must be the individual creation of each interim pastor, designed by that person to meet personal interests and needs. Certain aspects of the programs and services of APIMS and of IMN are personally supportive of interims and meet some of the characteristics of good support networks noted below. The intentional interim will find it worthwhile to join both organizations.

Support Networks for Interims

A good support network will have the following characteristics:

> It deals with a wide range of human needs, both personal and professional.
>
> It is set up deliberately and openly and describes definite parameters for support relationships.
>
> It is supportive and nourishing, never punitive or draining.
>
> It recognizes that identifiable skills are necessary and applicable to interim work, providing training opportunities as well as offering reasonable financial undergirding for professional development.
>
> It has connections not only in the congregation and the community but regionally and perhaps even nationally.

The interim pastor's personal relationships exist for many more reasons than just to provide support. Many truly healthy support relationships grow out of working connections in which there is constant giving and receiving. It is with this spirit of mutuality in mind that the following relationships are noted.

Governing Body Relationships

The presbytery, the session, the synod, and other governing bodies have particular and differing responsibilities for the entire interim pastor program and experience. Each should be acquainted with the tasks and opportunities that are theirs.

The Presbytery

The interim pastor will want to establish connections with the presbytery that build trust and are mutually productive. The initiative for this generally comes from the presbytery. Building trust, however, requires the energy and commitment of all parties to the relationship, and initiative for that may come from the interim as well as from the COM or others in the presbytery.

The interim pastor is one of the representatives from the pastoral arm of the presbytery to the congregation. This is part of the way the presbytery cares for its congregations. The interim should always endeavor to represent the presbytery as a concerned, caring community of which the congregation is a part. Especially when a pulpit vacancy occurs because a presbytery encourages a pastor to move, or results from presbytery discipline, it becomes imperative that the congregation experience the broader dimensions of the presbytery's supportive interest. The interim should be guided by the COM and the presbytery in all such matters affecting any aspect of the relationships between the session, the congregation, and the mission and ministry of the presbytery or the larger church. *Remember:* Specific advice from the presbytery will always supersede any suggestions in this manual.

Many church officers and members have little more than a vague concept of what a presbytery is and does, not realizing that the life and health of every congregation within its bounds is of real concern to the presbytery. Church leaders also need to know that the presbytery has a variety of resources to share with every congregation: staff persons, consultants, programs in leadership development, church education, stewardship, evangelism, mission, social justice, and so on.

Membership of the interim pastor in the presbytery is advisable, even though it is of short duration. In some presbyteries, membership is mandatory if the interim pastor is to be the moderator of the session. Close consultation with the COM is called for.

The Session

The moderator of the session of a church with a vacant pulpit is appointed by the presbytery upon recommendation of the COM. The interim pastor is usually designated as the moderator but, if not, would ordinarily be present and participate in session meetings anyway. When the interim pastor is a member of another presbytery, a clear working arrangement regarding his or her role with the session should be made with the moderator of the session and with the approval of the COM. Such a plan is always difficult in practice, which is why it is best if the interim is the session moderator.

The interim who is head of staff must be moderator to function efficiently. The interim associate attends session meetings and may moderate at the request of the moderator.

The Synod

Several synods now provide programs for training and support of interim pastors. Such programs vary in style and content: some are only brief introductions; others are more extended. Some are fully accredited and can lead to denominational recognition as a Certified Interim Minister. The General Assembly's Office of Certification and Accreditation in Churchwide Partnerships in the National Ministries Division can provide the names of those training programs that lead to certification. For the sake of improving the practice of interim ministry, such training programs should be encouraged. It would be wise to consult with the Office of Certification and Accreditation in establishing any training programs, even brief introductory programs (see Appendix A). If the COM chooses to require the use of certified interim pastors in its churches, it is the place of the COM to tell sessions and interim pastors where such programs exist and how best to make use of them.

The IMN offers a range of training programs, including some which lead to IMN certification for interim ministry. Some

Presbyterian pastors have chosen to attend these ecumenical programs because they are offered at different times and in different locations from the General Assembly or synod programs. The IMN and the General Assembly certification board, in general, recognize each other's programs and certification.

The General Assembly

In some congregations, interim pastors are given the privilege of attending the General Assembly each year. This time away from the congregation may be considered as service to the denomination or as part of one's study leave, and is not counted against vacation time. In some larger congregations, the interim pastor's General Assembly expenses are paid by the session or the congregation. When an interim is contracting with such a congregation, it may be appropriate to ask if this perquisite could be granted. Even a few days at a General Assembly will benefit the congregation, as well as the interim pastor, in a variety of ways. Such a visit is nearly always stimulating to a pastor, refreshing the mind as well as the spirit.

Attending the General Assembly also gives the interim a chance to relate more closely to an informal national network of persons interested in interim ministries. The APIMS staffs a booth at the Assembly exhibit hall each year which provides a place to make useful contacts. Sometimes interim placement opportunities develop at General Assembly. The benefits of attending the annual meeting are such that a number of interims attend regularly at their own expense.

Some interim pastors who undertake this work as a long-term vocational choice have expressed regret that serving as an interim often seems to rule out the possibility of ever being sent to a General Assembly by a presbytery. Presbytery nominating committees ought to consider occasionally nominating an interim pastor as a commissioner to the Assembly. This suggestion also applies to service on General Assembly entities or synod boards, committees, and divisions.

Ecumenical Relationships

The posture of the interim pastor in relating to the clergy of other congregations in the community is of consequence for the ongoing life of the congregation. As a Presbyterian pastor, the interim will usually have an ecumenical interest and, in exercising this, may want to learn what direction the congregation has taken in the past and what ecumenical relationships are important, advisable, or acceptable in the near future. The interim pastor will want to continue any customary local participation in ecumenical work or worship. Certainly the interim pastor will, in every appropriate way, engage in efforts to bring to fruition the prayer of our Lord for his disciples, "That they may all be one" (John 17:21).

10

The Interim Pastor's Spouse: Opportunity and Challenge

"Change is all around us—radical change—and women are at the heart of much of it . . . women are changing the church." Isabel Rogers, a former moderator of the General Assembly, made that statement in 1993 at the Women's Breakfast held at the General Assembly in Orlando, Florida. Dr. Rogers referred to a *Time* magazine cover story titled "The Second Reformation," which attributed some of the ferment in the churches to the ordination of women. She agreed, but added that all women in the church were involved, not just clergywomen.*

These changes have already brought significant benefits for both men and women in the church, including spouses of clergy. Before women were ordained in the Presbyterian Church, the wife of the pastor was often treated as an unordained and unpaid assistant. Her home was considered an annex to the church. Meetings and classes were often held there. Fortunately, this is now generally a thing of the past. Today, spouses of pastors have more freedom to be individuals, and spouses of interim pastors can be among the most free.

Interim pastors' spouses can usually continue their private personal lives, and their public church lives will be even freer than the spouses of installed pastors. This is true whether the spouse is male or female. Because everyone knows that the interim will be with them for only a limited time, fewer demands are made on the spouse. One result is that the spouse of an interim can readily experiment with different roles: a very limited role in one church, an active role in another. In yet another pastorate, the spouse may

Horizons, A Magazine for Presbyterian Women, November/December 1994: 32.

choose to be active only in community groups. And, the spouse who lives in a distant community may never, or only infrequently, participate in the interim pastor's church.

The husband of an interim pastor may well be the first male spouse of a pastor the congregation has known. For that reason alone, husbands of interims have more freedom to choose whatever role they want. With few models available, no one knows quite what to expect of a pastor's husband.

An interim pastor's spouse can make a real contribution to interim service, assuming a unique place in interim ministry. Sincere interest and a friendly response to members will do much to strengthen the life of the church at a difficult time in its history. Just being present in the congregation at worship or on social occasions is a witness in itself. Many will find additional ways to share in ministry.

What Does It Take?

Interim ministry involves constant change. Flexibility is helpful for the interim pastor and for the spouse as well. Self-assurance is an important asset, the ability to set limits, to make decisions, and to display confidence in one's decisions. It is essential for the spouse to be able to identify and express his or her own feelings as well as to understand and relate to the feelings of the interim. Vitality, good health, a positive attitude toward life, a lively sense of humor, and a strong spiritual base is of real assistance to the spouse of an interim pastor. Familiarity with the basic theory of interim ministry would be helpful for an interim pastor's spouse in understanding and supporting the work of the interim (see chapters 5 and 6).

With these basic principles in mind the spouse can choose what, if any, tasks to accept in the church. The spouse should not accept an elected leadership position on the session or the deacons. Such conflict of interest could delay the congregation's work on its developmental tasks, in particular the third task, allowing needed leadership changes.

Patterns for Interim Living

There are a number of possible living patterns for the interim pastor to consider. Husbands and wives are encouraged to review the suggestions in this manual, talk to some experienced interim pastors and their spouses, and work out a living arrangement that best suits their needs. They may experiment with different plans from time to time to discover the effect on their marriage, their home, their family, and the congregation. A good place to meet experienced people who can share their interim life stories is at an interim training event or at the annual meetings of the Interim Ministry Network (IMN) and the Association of Presbyterian Interim Ministry Specialists (APIMS). There may be experienced interim pastors in one's own presbytery, too.

Living arrangements for the couple called to interim service in the church fall into three main patterns: the accompanying spouse, the settled spouse, and the visiting spouse. Each has its advantages, and most churches are willing to accept whatever pattern the couple themselves choose.

The Accompanying Spouse

In this pattern the spouse travels with the interim pastor, helping to make a home in each new community. The couple may or may not have a home base or own a home. The quality of the temporary housing can vary greatly. In some places a manse may be available for interim use; at other times a house or an apartment must be rented. How much local help will be available for help with cleaning and settling in will also vary from place to place, as will assistance in hunting for a rental house or apartment. Frequently, parish committees or individuals in the church will offer such assistance. If a manse is used by the interim and spouse, it generally must be vacated in time to prepare for the incoming pastor.

The couple may or may not move furniture with them. If they move furniture, the spouse often takes the lead in making arrangements, packing and unpacking, and settling in each new home. The spouse can choose whether or not to work in each new community. This lifestyle is usually the most satisfying for the spouse who is not working outside the home or who seeks only temporary or part-time employment.

Although a few interim pastors have been able to take children when they move from one call to another, it is difficult to do so. Children generally do not thrive if they are moved every year or two. While it is true that military families have survived well with frequent transfers, the military is able to provide resources that the church cannot afford, which make a major difference in the impact this lifestyle has on the family. Occasionally, resourceful mothers and fathers have been able to surround their children with enough love, security, and stability so that they can flourish even with frequent moves. Few civilian families, however, are equal to the strains and stresses of such upheaval. Accompanying the interim is not recommended for families with growing children. Other living arrangements may be more appropriate: for example, commuter or regional interim lifestyles, which are discussed later in this chapter.

One spouse of an interim pastor who has had considerable experience in accompanying her husband on all his assignments is Joyce Cameron. She and her husband, Duncan, have moved frequently and widely across the country. Having led a number of programs for spouses at interim pastors' seminars at Montreat, North Carolina, Joyce has compiled the following insightful lists of positive and negative aspects of this interim lifestyle.

Positive Aspects

> Exciting new places
> Challenging new church groups
> Less worry about upkeep on one's home base
> Lots of new friends
> A possibly enhanced marriage
> Expanded trust in God
> No long-term commitments
> New opportunities to share skills and interests
> The chance to reassess one's lifestyle
> Less overall job pressure
> More time for personal interests

Negative Aspects

> Continual packing and unpacking
> No real home of one's own
> Poor-quality housing
> Househunting difficulties
> Leaving one's friends each year
> Stress of finding local services and recreation
> Expenses of constant moving
> Possible negative church or community environment

Problems in finding jobs
Uncertain income
No long-term church activity

Grief

Grief can be a major factor during an interim period. Both partners may regularly experience their own sense of loss at leaving
friends behind. At the same time, they may be dealing with the
grief of the new congregation over the departure of a beloved pastor. They may encounter distress over church conflict or a former
pastor's misbehavior. By the time the congregation has worked
through its pain and is beginning to feel some hope and joy once
more, interim pastor and spouse will once again be facing another
grief experience: their own departure.

It can be hard to establish any ongoing relationships in a short
time. Therefore, the spouse will want to consider all the suggestions in this chapter and follow those that are helpful. Failure to
find new friends and companions promptly in a new setting may
lead to depression. Adding to the anxiety is the uncertainty of finding the next call, of knowing what income will be provided, of
wondering what to do with a significant gap in employment.
There are, nonetheless, helpful ways to deal with all these problems. Many couples have weathered them successfully and continue to find satisfying rewards in interim service.

Keeping Busy

Interim ministry, with its conditions and obligations, is not for
the Lone Ranger. Commenting on her experience as the wife of
an interim pastor, one woman wrote, "You become closer to your
spouse because he is the only close person you have, but it is
lonely, especially for the wife." She also pointed out that the pastor is always very busy initially, while the spouse does not have
nearly as much to do once they have settled in. The spouse, therefore, needs to have some absorbing personal interests to structure
the time.

Joyce Cameron encourages spouses to join local classes, workshops, or volunteer organizations or to find temporary work.
There may be a presbytery committee or project to support or
classes to teach in the church or community. The interim's day off
can be used to explore the area together, visiting restaurants, his-

toric sites, parks, and museums. Local papers may list concerts, fairs, special programs, and other community news. And when the interim is busy, the spouse can invite someone else to lunch!

The accompanying spouse will probably take the lead in preserving family rituals that provide stability and pleasure in life. Because the couple is in a temporary home, many things need to be simplified. Still, a few traditions should be kept. Each family will know best what is important for them.

Support Groups

Spouses of interim pastors will find it rewarding to seek some kind of personal support group in each new presbytery. Best might be a group of spouses of other interims. The spouse may even want to take the initiative to form such a group if none exists. Occasionally, interim pastor groups include spouses. Others organize separate groups for spouses. In one presbytery, the two groups meet separately and join for lunch. In one synod, two smaller presbyteries form one common support group for interims and their spouses.

Other kinds of support systems might include a spiritual formation group for prayer or meditation, a book club, an athletic group, bowling or golf, or any other special interest.

Self-Care

The interim pastor and spouse should avoid going to a new position exhausted. The spouse may need to highlight the importance of having vacation time between each interim call; that should be part of the contract. The interim may need encouragement to ask for one to three months' severance pay at the end of each interim to make such a vacation possible.

During the vacation, and while "on duty" in each new place, the spouse and the interim will want to take time to be alone together, to listen to each other without always feeling the need to respond, to talk about the former church or churches (but not with any others present), to have fun, and to recognize grief and find ways to nurture each other.

Spiritual Nurturing

"One of the gifts of Interim Ministry for me is the opportunity to explore my spiritual journey as we move from one place to another," Joyce Cameron wrote in a personal letter. In working with spouses attending interim training, she constantly emphasizes the importance of spiritual nurturing, private study of scripture, spending time alone with God both in prayer and in journaling, and looking to God for direction in personal meditation and retreat. In addition, daily prayer time with husband and wife together is an important ritual, one that can be easily transported from place to place.

The interim pastor and spouse may need to look for special times and places to worship together, since the interim has so few opportunities to renew his or her spiritual reserves. "We sometimes go to a midweek service at another church or attend a special evening service. Feeding our spiritual needs is extremely important," Joyce Cameron concludes.

The Settled Spouse

When the interim pastor owns a home, when the spouse has a good job, when there are young children living at home, or when the spouse chooses not to be uprooted every twelve or fifteen months, that spouse may decide to stay settled while the interim pastor serves in other places. There are some obvious advantages for the spouse. He or she can keep a career or a good job intact. The children can remain in the same school. The partners are free to manage their own time. The settled spouse can be active in the home church and retain long-term friendships. Each partner can plan so that the time they have together is quality time. They may be more likely to do this if they know such time is limited.

Disadvantages are real too. There will be long stretches without seeing one's partner or family. Loneliness may turn into depression without careful attention to the spiritual and emotional needs of each spouse. The settled spouse does not share the interim experience and is therefore cut out of a significant dimension of the partner's life. The couple can too easily grow apart unless special precautions are taken. The expenses of maintaining two households, even if one is spartan, can be a real burden. (Under some circumstances the interim pastor may find that some or all of the expenses of maintaining a second household purely for business purposes are tax deductible, while still claiming the settled home as the minister's residence where many expenses are tax deductible. An interim pastor should not make such claims, however, without consulting a tax adviser. Certain conditions must be met to do this legally.)

When a couple is considering living apart for the duration of a particular interim, special provisions ought to be in the contract. Time for the interim to visit at home on a regular basis is important, and the spouse may want to visit the interim pastor some of the time. Expenses for those visits may be paid by the church as part of the contract.

Commuter Interims

A variation on the foregoing lifestyle may be called the *commuter interim*. In this case, the settled spouse stays home while the interim pastor commutes to the church. Under this pattern the interim may accept assignments either anywhere in the nation or only in a limited region, often within one presbytery. If the church or the interim pastor can achieve this lifestyle, it has all the advantages of the settled spouse and few disadvantages. There is, of course, the wear and tear of travel for the commuter. More distant commutes will involve airfare, which can put a strain on the budget. Interim pastors who have been able to secure such calls, nonetheless, are glad to make the commuter's sacrifices in order to keep the family at home. This is the style many younger interim pastors try to arrange for themselves and their families.

Some commuter interim pastors stay part of the week in the neighborhood of the church and go home on their days off. One made his temporary home in the church itself. Another stayed in guest rooms in the homes of church members. Some interims have been "house sitters" in the homes of church members on vacation. Creative pastors and church members have devised many ways to find temporary housing for the commuter interim pastor.

Regional Interims

Increasingly, interim pastors who live in large presbyteries are finding they can be constantly employed in interim service in one presbytery. They can enjoy all the benefits that living at home brings.

One question for the spouse of a regional interim pastor is, Where will the spouse worship? Some decide not to attend the church the interim is serving. Moving church attendance around the presbytery every few months can be confusing and unsatisfying.

Many spouses simply join one congregation and worship there no matter where the interim is at work. If the interim explains this to each session as the contract is negotiated, elders rarely object.

When the interim's work is confined to a limited region, there may be fewer options for jobs. To ensure employment, the pastor may want to accept short-term interim assignments or work in smaller churches. That can mean lower income. There may be, at times, longer periods of unemployment with less financial security. To address that problem, a few presbyteries have provided a minimum salary when the interim is unemployed. This is not common, however.

Other presbyteries have called interim pastors to be members of the presbytery staff. They are then "loaned" to churches in need of an interim. That church pays the presbytery for the interim's services. The presbytery, in turn, guarantees the pastor an ongoing salary and employment in some presbytery task when no interim congregation is available.

The Visiting Spouse

A few spouses of interim pastors have been able to combine the advantages of being an accompanying spouse with the advantages of being a settled spouse. When circumstances are right or can be adequately arranged, some spouses have been able to spend significant amounts of time with their partners even with considerable obligations at their home base. This is rare, but it is worth mentioning as a special category. If for no other reason, it encourages interim pastors and their spouses to consider breaking the mold, creating their own new life patterns, and changing them whenever and wherever the spirit leads.

Imagination is one of God's greatest gifts. Many of us do not exercise it sufficiently. A few have felt that their circumstances would not allow imaginative changes. To paraphrase what former General Assembly Moderator Isabel Rogers said at the General Assembly Women's Breakfast in Orlando, change is all around—radical change—and interim ministry is at the heart of much of it. Entering as fresh a field as interim ministry will open a wide range of exciting possibilities for both the wife and the husband who are willing to exercise their imaginations, putting together a new life for themselves in a new form of service to Christ's church.

11

Special Lifestyles and Concerns

The interim pastor's life has many significant differences from that of a settled pastor. First is the fact of high mobility for most interims. As one pastor said wryly, "This is a moving experience!" The interim in many cases must be the kind of person who either enjoys or at least can tolerate moving frequently. Indeed, not only one's household but the pastor's office must be moved each time there is a change of assignment.

Some experienced interim pastors believe it is highly advisable to have a home base to which to retreat for rest and recreation between assignments or during periods of unemployment. They suggest that this base be more or less permanent and easily accessible. Such an arrangement can be costly.

Others feel that this kind of a home base is not a necessity. They are able to manage satisfactorily not only their housing but their feelings about not having a permanent residence. There are ways to make constant moving acceptable, perhaps even fun for a time. Some suggestions have already been mentioned (see chapter 10).

Lifestyles

Interim pastors go about living and working in a wide variety of ways. Here are some examples.

A pastor, age 58, a widower, began doing interim service after deciding to shift gears professionally. In looking toward retirement, he built a home in a wilderness area that he made his permanent base. For several years he lived at home during the summer months, working as a wilderness guide and with governmental forest services. From October 1 to early May he took interim pastorates anywhere in the country.

Another pastor, at 45, had become a skilled troubleshooter. Then he and his family chose the interim route, taking eighteen-month contracts with particularly difficult, conflict-ridden congregations. In this case, he was often appointed as interim by administrative commissions of various presbyteries. He was probably the first interim to develop a contract calling for three months' terminal pay to cover the gaps between contracts. He had few problems finding challenging situations and used his skills for nearly twenty years.

Another pastor, who retired at 65, had completed eleven interim pastorates by the age of 77, most of them relatively brief— about six to eight months. He focused on maintaining the pastoral work of the congregation and did not touch the search process. He found it very satisfying to use his considerable personal and pastoral skills and do a good bit of traveling. His wife enjoyed the variety and travel, too.

One pastor, single and female, with a high degree of flexibility and mobility, soon learned how quickly to establish meaningful support relationships with congregations and communities. While building these new friendships, she learned that it is also important to maintain other permanent personal and therapeutic ties in order to provide an emotional and social balance during days of isolation and transition. For this minister, the interim pastorate was a conscious career choice made during seminary years, based in part on her hope that her interim work would increase the church's openness to women as installed pastors.

A black pastor who retired from service in a congregation in a large city was able to remain in his own home there. In his retirement he served so successfully as interim pastor in a strong white congregation in that city that they wanted to call him as their installed pastor. He declined, however, and continued to serve effectively as interim pastor in a variety of other congregations in that presbytery.

Another pastor, 55 and male, was a teacher in a metropolitan area. His interim tasks involved mostly weekend and evening work. Twice called to work in large and demanding congregations as an interim pastor, he found the work challenging and exciting, enabling him to use pastoral skills which he enjoyed but did not get to use every day.

A clergy couple (both husband and wife ordained as Ministers of the Word and Sacrament) found a congregation willing to call one of them as installed pastor. That church, however, was unable to offer a call to the partner. By working closely with the presbytery and synod concerned, the other pastor found a satisfying ministry in a series of interim assignments in congregations near the spouse's call.

Concerns

Marital Status

Do single persons find it harder to be effective and gratified as interim pastors? Definitely not! The single person is often more accustomed to making friends quickly. Furthermore, an interim has a ready-made network of friends among church officers and members of congregations and presbyteries. In addition, the single person often has fewer personal possessions to move and can sometimes make important decisions more quickly because no other member of the family has to be consulted. In many ways, the single person can adapt easily and quickly to the interim style of life.

Stability

The level of stability, both personally and professionally, of any interim pastor is always a matter of concern. People who are themselves in the midst of significant personal transitions may not work very well in transitional jobs. Some divorced or divorcing persons, for example, may be traumatized temporarily by their personal experiences; some congregations are, in a similar way, traumatized by the loss of their pastor. Obviously it would not be wise to call a traumatized person to a traumatized church. There are on record, nonetheless, a number of instances where recently divorced ministers have served very effectively as interim pastors. The key is for the committee on ministry (COM) and the session to know the candidate well and to make a careful match with an appropriate congregation. Stability is not directly related to marital status. The single, divorced, or widowed pastor can be fully as effective as the married one.

Financial Security

The personal financial program of an interim pastor is often considerably different from that of the installed pastor. It is important for the interim to plan this dimension of life carefully. In negotiating with the session or its personnel committee and the

COM, salary, pension, medical benefits, and all other details need to be very thoughtfully worked out. Moving expenses, both going to and returning from an interim assignment if that is necessary, ought to be settled as part of the initial agreement.

Another significant concern for those involved in interim service relates to providing for one's financial needs during the possible hiatus between assignments. Most interim pastors cannot be sure they will have a constant income. Further, the amount an interim is paid may vary widely from one church to another. If the pastor can build up some financial reserves, either before going into interim service or during such ministry, many problems can be alleviated. Another plan is to include in the contract provisions for transitional support. Such a plan provides salary continuance or, at the very least, minimal pension and major medical benefits or a Medicare supplement for a period from thirty to ninety days after the end of the interim if the pastor does not yet have employment.

Housing

Between assignments, the interim pastor may be without a place to live. It would be helpful if the interim had some established roots (a home or family or friends with whom to live), but many do not. This may seem a rather bleak picture of the interim's life, but a person who seriously considers this calling needs to take into account such a possibility. Single persons have found clergy friends with whom they could visit for a few weeks or months in between interims. Others have used this time to make long-delayed visits to sisters or brothers or other family members. Married couples have sometimes been able to visit their children during the times of freedom from employment.

Many pastors who have given a number of years in interim service find great joy in their work and consider the times between active interim calls to be, like sabbatical leaves, occasions for rest and rejoicing with family and friends. For them it is a most rewarding ministry.

Stress and Mobility

Recent studies have pointed out the high incidence of stress and burnout in nearly all the helping professions. This includes the ministry of the church, and interim work is one of the more uncertain and stressful forms of ministry. Frequent moves, the lack of job security, the absence of normal support systems, being subjected to a constant change of doctors, dentists, and community services, and the normal aggravations related to moving can be a source of real stress. As much as any installed minister and perhaps more, interim pastors need to pay attention to the level of stress in their lives and make conscious efforts to reduce it. Some books dealing with ministerial stress are listed in the bibliography.

Self-care in little ways as well as in major ones is essential. Effective time management is one form of self-discipline that interim pastors particularly need. In addition, proper diet, exercise, and rest can help reduce the negative impact of a high-stress lifestyle. Above all the interim pastor needs to develop a personal spiritual discipline in forms that can readily be practiced anywhere at any time. Personal meditation, worship, and journal writing can give any pastor a quality of character that makes life virtually burnout-proof.

One interim pastor, after describing a number of problems he had faced, added, "If the above sounds forbidding, I have overdrawn the picture. I have found that during my interimships I lived and worked under a great deal less pressure than during my pastorates. An interim pastor is not responsible for the introduction and nurture of long-term policies and programs. The interim is not as likely to be on call day and night as an installed pastor would be. Living accommodations will often be smaller and simpler than those of a manse. Consequently, the interim will not be expected or be able to do as much entertaining as an installed pastor." Clearly, for this pastor, part of his success in dealing with stress was his positive attitude toward his life circumstances.

Reentry into an
Installed Pastorate

Persons who have served one or more interim pastorates, and who are not retired, sometimes want to return to the status of an installed pastor, for a variety of personal reasons. The spouse may be weary of frequent moving. The interim may be equally worn out after ministering to a procession of church officers and members. Those who have come to this point generally find that returning to more traditional forms of ministry is not easy. Experienced interim pastors have pointed out that nearly all nonparish clergy and specialized ministers have a difficult time in finding a call to a parish position. Interim pastors are not much different.

Most pastor nominating committees (PNCs) want a pastor with fresh experience in a pastorate. They hesitate to call specialized ministers because they fear such ministers are out of touch with the parish. Sometimes a search committee seems to think that specialized ministers may have turned their backs on parish ministry when they entered their specialty service. Only by very careful and determined effort is it possible to persuade most PNCs otherwise, but it can be done.

Another element seems to work against the interim pastor who wants to return to an installed position. People generally distrust someone who moves around a lot. Moving every year (or more often) may give the impression that a pastor is undependable or lacks staying power. While pastors who have served only one interim may not have too much difficulty in returning to an installed position, the longer a person has been in interim service, the more difficult it is to return to an installed position as a parish pastor.

When an interim pastor expresses a desire to return to an installed position, all the resources of the presbytery, the synod, and the General Assembly should be made available. Relocation to a new position is seldom easy for any minister in the Presbyterian system, but diligent and careful search usually brings the desired reward. Success in such an effort means careful preparation of a new personal information form well before the search begins. If the regular system is used fully, and if other channels for reaching PNCs are also accessed, success will come. A number of other unwarranted stereotypes still work against the interim who wants to move to a settled position. Governing body executives and COM members will want to give careful attention to any interim who seeks to return to an installed position in the pastorate.

Retirement

The majority of interim pastors today are retired or close to retirement. Their years of experience have equipped them to deal easily and comfortably with many of the problems of the parish. Such pastors often have a maturity and depth of understanding that gives them the ability to handle effectively divisions in the congregation and hostilities among members and groups. Further, retired persons generally have only one dependent moving with them, and this is easier than uprooting an entire family every six to twelve months. In addition, retired persons often have pensions or supplemental income. They can accept service where there is only modest remuneration.

At present well over three thousand ministers in the Presbyterian Church (U.S.A.) are listed as honorably retired. Of this number, there are those for whom age or health makes it impossible to serve in any professional capacity. Others, however, are finding interim ministry offers a very satisfying way to continue in service to the church.

Serving a church as an interim can provide a way in which to continue a fruitful ministry without the strains and pressures of a full-time pastorate. The ministry is a demanding calling, and thirty or forty years in it often leaves a person exhausted, whether the individual has served as a pastor, teacher, missionary, evangelist, an administrator, or in some other position. Still, the retired minister may not want to stop entirely. Interim service can be for three to six months of the year, leaving time for travel, recreation, writing, and other pursuits.

Retired persons who are serving as interim pastors need to be particularly careful about pension and Social Security benefits. Certain provisions in the Internal Revenue Service Code and court rulings can mean significant savings in a minister's income tax if the right arrangements are made in each interim assignment. The goal of every loyal citizen is to pay the IRS every dollar that is owed but not one penny more! The Board of Pensions will send on request a free income tax guide for ministers. It is clear, helpful, and well worth studying.

Today there are good retirement provisions ably administered under the pension plan, coupled with provision for Medicare supplements, experience apportionments that work almost like cost of living increases, and other benefits. For many Presbyterian ministers, there is not as much financial pressure as there used to be for a minister to try to stay active longer. Interim pastor service can be a dependable source of additional income for a time, however, if needed or desired.

Pensions and
Postretirement Service

Retired members of the Presbyterian pension plan may serve any other Presbyterian church or employing organization while receiving a retirement pension. The pension board allows two types of postretirement service:

1. Service of up to twelve months as an interim or stated supply, if the church is seeking a full-time pastor. Twelve percent postretirement service dues, sometimes called "vacancy dues," are paid by the church on the former minister's effective salary.

2. Service to a "small" church, to a "divided" church, or in a part-time position with no restrictions on the amount of time served. Twelve percent postretirement dues are paid by the church on the total effective salary of the retired member of the pension plan.

If there are any questions about whether or not a particular position is type 1 or type 2 as described, queries should be directed to the nearest regional pension representative or to the Board of Pensions Office. Current addresses and phone numbers for these offices are listed in the Presbyterian Planning Calendar each year.

There has been increasing interest in early retirement. With interim service as a viable option, many ministers may find this a desirable choice. Interim work enables a retired person to visit, serve, and live for a while in various parts of the church. A few interims have achieved remarkable success in spending the summer in the northern parts of the church and the winter in Florida or on the Gulf Coast. Such good fortune is unusual, of course, and one should not enter interim service for that reason alone.

The best way to hold off the encroachments of aging, we are told, is to remain as mentally and physically active as possible. Nothing ages a person so much as just quitting or slowing down to a crawl. Most of us can maintain good health better by engaging in some productive work for the Lord. Interim service is not the only way to do this, but it is one of the better ways.

In some observations he made several years ago, Edward W. Ziegler, one of the early Presbyterian interim pastors, wrote to a friend, "For some retired ministers the interim relationship is an answer to prayer. Thus far, it has been my privilege to serve in that capacity in two churches, one in the East and one in the Midwest. I recommend this form of ministry to any retired pastor who is reasonably healthy, loves people, is adaptable to new situations, is receptive to new ideas, still feels a tingle of excitement when confronted by problems and opportunities which so often go hand in hand, and who does not mind a bit of moving about." After he wrote that note, Ziegler served almost another decade in interim ministry, much to the benefit of several congregations and his own sense of personal worth and joy.

12

The Growing Edge of Interim Ministries

Several Protestant denominations have been experimenting for more than twenty years with a number of carefully organized intentional approaches to a variety of interim ministries. Efforts have been focused chiefly, however, in the interim pastorate.

Significant progress has been made in both the theory and the practice of interim ministry on the initiative of the Alban Institute, the Interim Ministry Network (IMN), and many denominational organizations, including the Association of Presbyterian Interim Ministry Specialists (APIMS). Training, advocacy, and developmental programs have been spawned by these and other groups. The Episcopal Church, the Lutherans, the United Church of Christ, the Disciples of Christ, the American Baptists, and the United Church of Canada have been leaders in the expansion of this movement. Churches in Australia and New Zealand have also begun to employ interim pastors and have turned to some of the American churches for guidance. A few Roman Catholic Church leaders are studying the possibility that they might employ interim pastors or consultants to serve in parishes with special problems, particularly clergy misconduct cases.

Until recently, the denomination with the largest number of pastors practicing interim ministry was the Presbyterian Church (U.S.A.). Presbyterians have had the largest number of members in the IMN since its inception.

The concept of a specialized interim ministry is now well established and the movement is beginning to enter another phase, expanding into additional fields of service and influence. The developing strength of the IMN and the creation of APIMS and similar groups among Lutherans and Episcopalians are further indications of the growing strength of the interim ministry movement.

Many presbyteries have now adopted the policy, rare only a few years ago, that every church seeking a new pastor must employ a trained, intentional interim pastor. Several presbyteries have employed at least one full-time intentional interim pastor who is considered a member of the presbytery's paid staff but whose only assignment is to serve as interim pastor of congregations seeking an installed pastor. The trend is growing, and more governing bodies are planning to call resident interim pastors.

Interim Executives

In another development, presbyteries and synods are now generally employing intentional interim ministry specialists as interim executives when the head of staff or associate executives of the governing body retire or move to other positions. Experience indicates that the dynamics of a transition in leadership in the presbytery or synod are much the same as in a congregation.

The Reverend Joan Mabon, who served in several interim executive positions, has written in the *Presbyterian Outlook:*

> When a governing body loses executive staff, this body . . . like any other system of relationships . . . is faced with a number of new concerns. The body as a whole needs to say good-bye to the departing executive, to honor that person's gifts . . . to deal with anxiety about maintaining present mission objectives. . . . An Interim Executive can offer a governing body the time to manage the awesome tasks at hand as well as the opportunity to celebrate and learn from the past before they are pushed too soon into the future. . . . An Interim Executive can offer the governing body's churches a model for using the interim period fruitfully. As more and more presbyteries and synods begin to encourage congregations to seek interim leadership, that encouragement is far more persuasive if the governing body itself can demonstrate commitment to this concept.

When a governing body shows that it, too, is . . . deeply
concerned for the relationships that are a part of its
very body, then its intention for strong interim ministry is believable.

Other forms of specialized ministry throughout the church are
also beginning to tap into the interim theory, learnings, and practical experience that have proved so valuable to congregations.
Synods, presbyteries, and committees on ministry (COM) would
be wise to begin now to consider these additional ways in which
interim ministry specialists can be employed to advance the mission of the church in their areas. One interim pastor in Houston
has pointed out several ways in which interim ministry can expand.
Some of his suggestions follow.

Interim Educators

Directors of Christian education, serving as interim educators
in a congregation or on a governing body staff, can be of major assistance while a search process is under way for a permanent staff
person. The intentional interim educator who understands the
special significance of the interim time, and who is willing to make
a commitment to use that opportunity to guide change, development, and reconciliation, can make a major contribution to the future health and strength of a governing body or a congregation.
Such persons can be of equal value to congregations, presbyteries,
synods, and General Assembly offices. College, university, and
seminary professors and administrators can also serve in special
roles to meet unique interim needs of the institution.

Interim Chaplains

Hospitals, nursing homes, sanitariums, rehabilitation centers,
prisons, halfway houses, and many other kinds of caregiving organizations are making effective use of a chaplain's services. The
chaplain with a firm grasp of interim theory and the interim
leader's special tasks can be of significant service to any of these
institutions and their programs when guided change, sensitive
maintenance, or reconciliation are needed in special circumstances for limited periods of time.

Interim Administrators

Executive or associate executive administrators can serve in any of the churches' mission or ministry offices and programs, in the various councils of churches and other ecumenical alliances, or in church-related or church-approved secular or government service programs. Presbyteries and their COMs will find that recognizing the validity of these newer forms of ministry, including interim specialists in these fields, will greatly strengthen the church and its mission and will provide new fields of service for many specialized ministers.

Interim theory and practice as they relate to transition and managed change are the subject of continuing study and experiment in the academic community and in the business world as well as in the church. More and more institutions are experimenting with this form of leadership for managing change.

Other Specialized
Interim Ministries

A brief study of the Acts of the Apostles, especially the opening chapters, will remind the reader of just how innovative and energetic the early church leaders were in their own response to the ministry and mission Christ had given them. The Gospels, too, reflect a band of disciples ready to invent new forms, to reinterpret traditional ways, and to follow their Lord wherever his ministry took them or sent them. Our contemporary church must learn to be as open and creative, tolerant and discerning, yet patient and caring as were those first followers of Jesus. Interim pastors are teaching the church a new way of looking at its life, especially in times of transition. Seldom has the church faced a more volatile time than at present.

The church's strength and future growth are, as always, in the hands of its own people, inspired and supported by Jesus Christ, the foundation and chief cornerstone. A wider, more informed, flexible, and intentional use of interim ministry in new fields of service is one way not only to sustain the kingdom of God on earth but to bring to it both reconciliation and new life and growth.

Appendix A:
The Interim Pastor
Certification Process

Presbyterian Church (U.S.A.)
National Ministries Division
Presbyterian Interim Ministry
Certification Board (PIMCB)

Purpose of Certification

Certification represents a judgment on the part of the Certification Board that a candidate has completed the required level of training, demonstrates the ability to articulate and apply interim theory, has functioned effectively in at least two interim positions, and has made a commitment to continued training, growth, and accountability. The purpose is to raise the level of professionalism in the field of interim ministry and to help presbyteries and congregations in their choice of effective pastoral leadership for the critical interim time.

*Appropriate Candidates
for Certification*

Those ministers who intend to continue in intentional interim service for a significant length of time as a career track will find certification appropriate for them. Those pastors who are practicing interim ministry during retirement or as a temporary position before returning to permanent calls will find that the time required for preparation and presentation of criteria most likely does not warrant the effort and expense of seeking certification. Many persons practice interim ministry with high standards without being certified.

Training and Experience Prerequisites

1. A two-week sequence of basic training in interim ministry theory and skills in a setting approved by the PIMCB (60 contact hours).
2. A field work project in some aspect of interim ministry under an approved supervisor. The field work may not begin until basic training is completed and lasts six months. The list of approved supervisors is included in the application packet.
3. Completion of two interim pastorates, one of which has been full time and both of which have been of nine or more months' duration.
4. Identification of additional continuing education experience related to interim ministry.
5. Current memberships in the Association of Presbyterian Interim Ministry Specialists (APIMS) and the Interim Ministry Network (IMN).

Evaluations
(Forms provided in packet)

1. From the clerks of session of the applicant's two most recent interim ministry assignments (one of which should be full-time).
2. From the executives of the presbyteries of the same two interim assignments. (The executive may choose to delegate completion of the evaluation to another staff person or committee on ministry (COM) official who has a closer knowledge of the applicant's work.)
3. From the field work supervisor.

Note: The applicant shall collect all of these evaluations and use them as a partial basis for the narrative report, then forward them with the application.

Application Form **and**
Narrative Information
(Forms provided in packet)

1. Application information.
2. The applicant's reflections on ethical issues faced in interim ministry and on the strengthening of relationships between congregations and higher governing bodies during the interim time.
3. Description of learnings garnered from the applicant's experience.
4. The deadlines for filing applications are May 1 and October 1 each year.

Interview

An important part of the process is a face-to-face interview with the Certification Board. A primary purpose is to assure the Board of the applicant's capacity to clearly discuss interim ministry theory and relate it to practice.

All of the application papers will have been carefully reviewed by Board members before the interview.

Interviews will occur twice each year when the Board is in session, usually late spring and late autumn. No interviews will be granted outside these settings. The applicant is responsible for the cost of travel, meals, and lodging necessary to attend an interview. After the application is filed, the applicant will be contacted concerning the scheduling of the interview.

Decision Making

Following receipt of all material, along with the application fee and the results of the interview, the PIMCB will make a recommendation regarding certification. The Board has three possible recommendations for each applicant: grant certification; deny certification; withhold certification. The decision of the Board will be communicated by letter. All information is kept in confidence by the Board.

If certification is withheld, the applicant will receive a notice of the Board's reasons. Also included will be suggestions or requests for future study, work experience, or other activity which may increase the applicant's chances for future certification. The application file will remain open for up to two years to allow for further work and a second interview without additional application fees.

This process is designed to enhance the quality and integrity of this specialized form of pastoral ministry. Your interest is appreciated. For an application packet or additional information, please contact PIMCB, Room M003, 100 Witherspoon Street, Louisville, KY 40202–1396; phone: 502-569-5751.

Appendix B:
Securing an Interim Pastor*

1. The committee on ministry (COM) representative meets with the session to outline options for pastoral leadership during the interim period.
2. The session makes a request to the COM to establish the interim position.
3. The COM authorizes the session to proceed.
4. The session personnel committee develops a position description and determines salary range and other terms of service.
5. The session approves the personnel committee's recommendations.
6. The COM critiques and approves the session's plans.
7. The session personnel committee, or the special interim search committee with COM guidance, seeks an interim pastor through presbytery and synod staff, the Call Referral System in the National Ministries Division, Association of Presbyterian Interim Ministry Specialists (APIMS), and faculty for various interim training programs.
8. The search committee does initial screening of personal information forms (PIFs), conducts interviews, and may hear interim pastor preach.
9. The session interviews the recommended interim pas-

---

*This process is based on suggestions in *The New Committee on Ministry Handbook*, 1994 edition, pp. 63–64.

tor, makes a decision, and requests approval of the COM.

10. The search committee or the session negotiates contract/covenant with the interim pastor for final approval by the session, the interim, the COM, and the presbytery.

11. The session notifies the congregation and plans for an appropriate service of recognition (*not* installation) and reception.

Appendix C:
A Suggested
Interim Pastor Contract

The following contract between the session of _____
Church and the Rev. _____ is for the purpose of providing
interim pastoral services to _____ Church. The session, being satisfied with Pastor _____'s qualifications and trusting
that his/her ministry in the Gospel will be to our spiritual benefit,
hereby commits our congregation to the following Covenant with
this pastor:

The Rev. _____ is invited to be interim pastor, full-time
or part-time (specify percent if part-time), of _____ Church.
[*Any statement relating to the ordination of the pastor and/or transfer
to the presbytery if not a member would be inserted here.*]

The Interim Pastor:

Will/will not become (is) a member of _____ Presbytery.

Will/will not serve as moderator of the session.

Will/will not serve as head of staff.

Will/will not assist the presbytery consultant in the conduct
of the mission study. If so, in what way?

Will/will not assist in preparation of the Church Information
Form. If so, how?

The interim pastor will be responsible for providing pastoral
duties as indicated in the following position description, which
shall include provision for evaluation. [*Suggestions for writing a position description are available from the presbytery office or the committee on ministry (COM). The following are examples only:*]

Lead worship and preach _____ Sundays per month.

Provide for a leader of worship on Sundays not present.

Make pastoral calls on sick and shut-ins as time permits.

Officiate at weddings, baptisms, and funerals as requested.

Plan and moderate session and congregational meetings.

Guide the session and congregation in their work on the five developmental tasks. [*They may be listed here.*]

Work with boards and committees to assist them in carrying out their assigned tasks.

Train newly elected officers in conjunction with staff and experienced church officers.

Perform other administrative duties as requested: e.g., work with church secretary in preparing bulletins and newsletters, exercise general oversight of church facilities, and represent the church in dealing with outside organizations.

Note: Duties as spelled out should be consistent with the full- or part-time status of the candidate. It may be useful to add: The normal work week will be _____ hours per day and _____ days per week. *Another form some sessions or COMs are using is:* The normal full-time work week will be 10 [or 12 or 13] modules per week. [*A module is one morning or afternoon or evening, each module being a minimum of two to three hours.*]

Goals for this ministry shall be [*some examples follow*]:

Maintenance of a healthy congregational life.

Continuity of pastoral leadership.

Development of short-range goals identified in the goal-setting process of the church.

Preparation of the congregation for the arrival of a new pastor.

During the length of the agreement, the Rev. _____ will be accountable to the presbytery through the COM. At the end of the contract, the session will provide a performance review. It is understood that should the Interim Pastor have any serious difficulties with any former pastor(s) of this congregation, the matter will be referred to presbytery's COM.

The Rev. _____:

Agrees not to be involved in any way with the pastor nominating committee (PNC), except to see that it makes adequate reports to the church. Any suggestions the interim pastor has regarding the PNC are to be submitted to the COM. [*Or:* The Rev. _____ will serve the pastor nominating committee in the following ways: *describe.*]

Agrees not to be a candidate for the position of installed pastor of _____ Church and in every way will seek to prepare for the coming of another as installed pastor.

This agreement is for a period of _____ months (not more than twelve: *Book of Order*, G-14.0513b) from the date below. This agreement may be terminated by the session upon 60 days' written notice. The interim pastor may terminate the agreement with 60 days' written notice and forfeiture of any payment beyond the 60-day period. This agreement may be extended in _____ month periods if all parties to the contract concur.

Terms: The Interim Pastor is employed on a full-time [or part-time; *specify percent of time*] basis, serving approximately _____ hours per week [or modules per week], and will be compensated for interim pastoral services as follows:

Base salary: $ _____

Housing allowance: [*Any statement concerning manse or any special housing arrangements shall be included here.*]

Full pension: $ _____

Car allowance: [*Include any statement involving travel on the job. The amount for car allowance should equal mileage plus depreciation.*]

Medical care: [*Retired persons are not covered for Major Medical expenses under the pension plan. They may have Medicare and a Medicare Supplement plan from the Board of Pensions. Some provision may be needed here for covering deductible medical expense for both retired and non-retired pastors.*]

Moving costs: [*Costs to and from the field can be specified in terms of the total actual cost or a maximum allowable dollar amount.*]

Vacation: To be earned at the rate of 1 week per quarter and used each quarter (*or accumulated as agreed on*).

Study leave: Two weeks annually [*including financial assistance consistent with the congregation's provision for the most recent installed pastor or according to presbytery's standards*].

Any released time provisions for special commitments and any other conditions of service shall be listed. [*This may include service to the presbytery, synod, or General Assembly and ecumenical church or community service.*]

Salary continuation contingency: Full salary and allowances shall be paid the interim pastor as necessary, not to exceed a period of three months beyond the end of the interim pastor's service to this congregation or the date of reemployment, whichever is earlier. This does not include such vacation and study leave as may be due at the time of termination. [*An alternate plan for smaller churches is to provide coverage of pension and medical care benefits as necessary, not to exceed three months beyond the end of the interim pastor's service.*]

Appendix D:
An Interim Pastor
Covenanting Service

Recognition of the new interim pastor's position and responsibility is helpful to the congregation as well as to the session. The liturgy suggested here has been used effectively in several churches, and something like it is recommended for every congregation employing an interim.

Participants in this ceremony usually include a representative of the committee on ministry (COM) or of the presbytery, the clerk of session, and/or the personnel committee chairperson. At times a minister or layperson representing the local association of churches or clergy council is invited to share in the ceremony, especially if this service is held in the afternoon or evening. The service that follows is designed to be used as part of the first Sunday worship service at which the interim pastor or the interim associate pastor appears.

Often some symbols appropriate to the interim tasks are given and received as part of the ceremony. This service suggests that the interim pastor bring a walking stick as a symbol of the itinerant calling and the brevity of the interim's stay. In another ceremony the interim associate pastor brought a backpack containing significant symbols of work with the church youth. The interim's own imagination may suggest other symbols. Keys to the church building are the usual symbol given to the interim by the session representative.

The Covenanting Ceremony

Session Representative:

In the name of the Lord Jesus Christ, the great head of the church, we are gathered here to affirm a covenant which we, the people of this congregation, have with our God, with the Presbytery of _____, and with one another. We are here also to constitute a new covenant relationship with our interim pastor, the Rev. _____. In creating this new covenant, the Presbytery is represented by _____ [*name and position of representative*]. The session of our congregation is represented by myself as clerk and by Elder _____, chair of our personnel committee.

Presbytery Representative:

It is my privilege as _____ [*name position*] of your presbytery to lead you in affirming our covenant of faith as congregation, presbytery, and interim pastor.

Session Personnel Chairperson:

We are met together this day to welcome and affirm the Rev. _____ as our interim pastor. Our session has carefully selected and enthusiastically invited him/her to provide spiritual leadership, pastoral care, and administrative oversight to our congregation during this time of transition. He/she has been blessed with a call from Christ and with particular skills, training, and experience in interim ministry. Speaking on behalf of the session of this congregation, I am pleased to present the Rev. _____ as our interim pastor.

Presbytery Representative:

As _____ [*name of position of representative*] of the Presbytery of _____ [*name*], and speaking for the Presbytery's committee on ministry, I am pleased to confirm that we have examined the pastoral credentials and experience of the Rev. _____. We have inquired into his/her preparation and performance in ministry, especially as an interim ministry specialist. We have also read his/her statement of faith, and we have welcomed the Rev. _____ as a member of this presbytery. Therefore, we affirm your selection of him/her and encourage you to covenant with him/her as your interim pastor and as your friend and guide in ministry.

Clerk or Personnel
Chair of Session:

The session, in a formal action at a regular meeting, has promised to look to the Rev. _____ as our pastor for this interim period. The elders have also committed themselves to undertake the special tasks of leadership that belong to them and to the congregation during this "in-between time." We have agreed to search for Christ's direction for the future of this church, to examine who we are and what our mission is, to support and pray for our pastor nominating committee when they are elected, and to prepare for and welcome the next installed pastor of this church.

Presbytery Representative:

A covenant is a promise of faith and practice, sealed by the grace of God. _____ [*name of interim pastor*], do you, before God and in the presence of these witnesses, commit yourself to this new trust and responsibility as interim pastor of _____ Church?

Interim Pastor:

I do.

Presbytery Representative:

Do you understand that you cannot be a candidate for an installed pastoral position in this congregation?

Interim Pastor:

I understand, and I will not be a candidate for an installed pastoral position in this congregation.

Presbytery Representative:

Will you serve the people of _____ Church with energy, intelligence, imagination, and love?

Interim Pastor:

I will.

Session Representative:

The congregation is now requested to answer these questions: Do you acknowledge and welcome the Rev. _____ as interim pastor of our congregation? If you agree, please reply, "We do."

Congregation:

We do.

Session Representative:

Do you, the members of this congregation, agree to undertake the special tasks that will be yours through this "in-between time," to pray for and encourage our interim pastor and our pastor nominating committee, when elected, and to welcome our new installed pastor when that person is found? If you agree, please reply, "We do."

Congregation:

We do.

Personnel Chairperson:

_____ [*name of interim pastor*], please accept these keys to this church building as a token of our commitment to you as our interim pastor. Use them as you serve us this year, and return them as you depart after you have helped us prepare for the future and for our new installed pastor.

Interim Pastor:

Thank you, _____, _____, _____ [*names of participants in ceremony*], and thank you, elders, deacons, and all members of this congregation. May our God bless and guide us as we work together on the special tasks that are ours now. _____ [*name of clerk*], please hold in trust for me this walking stick, which I brought with me this morning. It is a sign of the temporary interim nature of my ministry here. When I leave, please return it to me, so that I may carry it as I walk on to my next interim congregation.

Presbytery Representative:

And now may God's love and mercy surround and uphold this interim pastor, this session, and this congregation so that when their tasks are completed, each one may hear our Lord say, "Well done, good and faithful servant." Amen. [*It is appropriate that all leaders in this ceremony greet and welcome the interim pastor as the congregation sings a brief hymn of the church.*]

Appendix E:
The Process of Change

In *Changing Pastoral Leadership*, Loren B. Mead describes Project Test Pattern's work in four case studies of parishes that were provided with outside parish development adviser/consultants in order to assist in the change process. While these consultants were not interim pastors, much of their work was related to the interim's tasks. From those experiences, Mead isolated the following four learnings about congregations:

1. Congregations can change.
2. Congregations have a history that influences the change process.
3. Congregations are unique, and the model must be adapted for each situation.
4. The ways in which people relate to each other, information is communicated, and decisions are made have great power in shaping a congregation.

He also isolated five learnings about the process of change in congregations:

1. Third-party consultation can increase the rate of effectiveness of change in a congregation.
2. Covenant/contract relationships between parish and consultants must be carefully spelled out.
3. The pastor's own commitment to change will be a key to the extent to which a congregation will change.

4. Consultants, pastors, and congregations need support systems to help them handle anxieties related to change and uncertainty.
5. We can learn much from failures if we are open to examining them.

Finally, Mead makes the point that renewal is not a program; it is a process. As such, it is properly part of the ongoing life of the congregation and is not delimited by any single experience or effort.

Appendix F:
Outline of the
Conflict Intensity Chart*

Level One:
A Problem to Solve

There is real disagreement, conflicting goals, values, and needs. Anger is short-lived. Conflict tends to focus on the problem, not on personalities. There is open sharing of information. Language is clear and specific. The goal is to solve the problem and to move toward unanimous agreement, using a collaborative style. A win/win solution is possible.

Level Two:
A Disagreement

Participants do not agree on the definition of the problem, personalities mix with issues, and distrust begins. Some information is held back. Shrewdness and calculation appear. Language becomes more general and barbed. The goal now is not just to solve the problem but to save face. A win/win solution is still possible.

Level Three:
A Contest

The dynamic is now win/lose. Conflict is personalized; others are the enemy, and personal attacks and distortion of the problem are common. The goal is more complex and shifts from self-protection to winning. Mediation, compromise, and voting may work, but possibly some will leave the church.

*Adapted from *The New Committee on Ministry Handbook*, 1994, p. 166.

Level Four:
Fight or Flight

Factions are now solidified, with clear leaders. Each group believes the others cannot change and wants to hurt them and eliminate them from the church. Cold self-righteousness pervades every scene. There is a high probability that a significant number of members will leave.

Level Five:
An Intractable Situation—"War"

The issue is no longer clear. Personalities have become the issue. The conflict is now unmanageable. Behavior is vindictive and people cannot control their emotions. The goal is no longer to exile but to destroy the offending party or parties; for example, to see that the fired pastor never gets a job in any other church. The outcome will be highly destructive. An outside force, such as an administrative or judicial commission, will be necessary to make peace.

Appendix G:
Review and
Evaluation Processes

These review and evaluation processes (and the forms that follow) may be adapted to a wide variety of churches and pastors. In most cases, the interim pastor will need to take the lead. The situation in the individual congregation determines when and how to evaluate. The review of the interim pastor should take place at a different meeting from the review of the session's performance. If the elders have had an opportunity ahead of time to complete the review forms, the entire process will be more productive. A representative of the committee on ministry (COM) may be invited to observe or participate at either or both reviews.

Process for Review and Evaluation
of an Interim Pastor's Performance

The interim pastor review and evaluation may take place at one or more of the following intervals: three months, six months, or twelve months. In most churches the session itself will participate in the review under the leadership of the elder who is chairperson of the session personnel committee. In churches with a large number of elders on the session, it may be best to conduct the review only with the members of the personnel committee. The interim pastor is excused from the session room during the review of his or her performance. The discussion of each category should be limited to about five minutes. Ordinarily, the results of the review are shared with the interim pastor at another time and place, usually at a meeting of the personnel committee or in a conversation between the interim pastor and the personnel committee chairperson.

Process for Review and
Self-Evaluation of the Session

When the termination date of the interim pastor's service has been finally set (ordinarily about sixty days before the interim pastor's departure) it is advisable for the session to set a date and time for a review and evaluation of the session's performance during the interim period. The interim pastor should preside at this meeting, and the deliberations and conclusions may be recorded in the session minutes if that is desired.

Each elder should be encouraged to complete the evaluation form and bring it to the meeting for personal guidance during the discussion. The forms ought not to be collected or preserved. Each is regarded as the personal property of the person who has completed it. The results of the session review should be recorded, shared with the interim pastor, and used as the session itself decides.

Interim Pastor's Performance Review
(To be completed by each elder)

Interim Pastor's Name: _____ Date: _____

This form, to be completed by each elder, should be adapted appropriately for each situation. Its objective is to provide the interim pastor with performance feedback from the session.

The following questions concerning the performance of the interim pastor are to be addressed by the session in each performance category:

1. What was expected of the interim pastor in the performance period under review?
2. What strengths has the interim pastor exhibited?
3. What are the opportunities for growth and improvement?

Performance Categories (Consult the interim pastor's job description)	Meets or Exceeds Expectations	Growth Opportunity
INTENTIONAL INTERIM LEADERSHIP		
Guides the session and other leaders in these tasks:		
Coming to terms with history		
Discovering a new identity		
Allowing and empowering new leaders		
Renewing denominational linkages		
Commitment to new leadership and a new future		
Examples and comments:		

(continues)

(continued)

Performance Categories (Consult the interim pastor's job description)	Meets or Exceeds Expectations	Growth Opportunity
WORSHIP		
Worship services—primary leader and coordinator		
With the session and its worship committee, determines policies relating to the worship services		
Study, preparation, and preaching of sermons		
Administration of the sacraments		
Examples and comments:		
TEACHING		
Primary responsibility for the confirmation classes		
Coordination and teaching/leading adult Christian education events		
Support of Christian education for children and youth		
Examples and comments:		
PASTORAL CARE		
Prayer with and for the church		
Visitation of the sick, troubled, and grieving		
Officiating at funerals, along with preparatory and follow-up visits with the family		

(continues)

(continued)

Performance Categories (Consult the interim pastor's job description)	Meets or Exceeds Expectations	Growth Opportunity
PASTORAL CARE *(continued)*		
Weddings: premarriage counseling and officiating		
Pastoral care and counseling for troubled church members		
Examples and comments:		
COMMUNITY SERVICE		

Active in the local clergy association,
    lay/clergy counsel, ecumenical groups,
    and community service organizations		

Examples and comments:		
DENOMINATIONAL SERVICE		

Active in presbytery, synod, and
    General Assembly as invited
    and as time allows		

Supportive of the national and worldwide mission of the church		
Examples and comments:		

(continues)

Performance Categories (Consult the interim pastor's job description)	Meets or Exceeds Expectations	Growth Opportunity
STAFF LEADERSHIP		
Coordinator of volunteer and paid church staff		
Examples and comments:		
CHURCH LEADERSHIP		
Equip and encourage the members of the church to develop and use their gifts for ministry		
Moderate session and congregational meetings		
Attend session committee meetings in ex officio capacity		
Work with the session and its committees to develop and envision long-range plans for the congregation		
Primary responsibility for officer training		
Examples and comments:		

Elder's Personal Review and Self-Evaluation

Elder's Name: _____ Date: _____

This form is to be used by each elder to review his or her own performance during the interim period, as well as to review the performance of the session as a whole.

The following questions concerning performance are to be considered before completing this form:

1. What was expected of the elder/session during the interim period?
2. What strengths have the elders exhibited?
3. What are the opportunities for growth?

Other categories may be added to this form as indicated by the situation.

The Five Tasks:	Individual Elder			Whole Session		
	Well Done	Partially Done	Not Done	Well Done	Partially Done	Not Done
1. Coming to terms with history						
Examples and comments:						
2. Discovering a new identity						
Examples and comments:						
3. Allowing and empowering new leaders						
Examples and comments:						

(continues)

(continued)

The Five Tasks:	Individual Elder			Whole Session		
	Well Done	Partially Done	Not Done	Well Done	Partially Done	Not Done
4. Renewing denomin- ational linkages						
Examples and comments:						
5. Commitment to new leadership and a new future						
Examples and comments:						

Additional comments:

Appendix H:
A Farewell to
the Interim Pastor

Part of the congregation's work on its fifth developmental task, commitment to a new leader, is to say farewell to the interim pastor. A formal ceremony during the interim pastor's last worship service with the congregation will greatly assist that process. There may be someone present to represent the committee on ministry or the presbytery, but that is not as important now as it was at the beginning of the interim period. The following service suggests that two elders conduct this ceremony, perhaps the clerk and the chairperson of the personnel committee. Others may also be involved, if desired. The interim pastor will want to adapt and personalize what is suggested here.

The Farewell Ceremony

Clerk:

In the name of the Lord Jesus Christ, the great head of the church, we are gathered here today to affirm the continuing covenant which we, the people of _____ Church, have with our God, with the Presbytery of _____, and with one another. We are also here to dissolve the covenant relationship we have had with our interim pastor, the Rev. _____. I speak to you as clerk of the session, and joining me in our farewell is the chairperson of our personnel committee, _____ [*name*].

Personnel Chairperson:

It is with rejoicing and with regret that we come this day to thank the Rev. _____ for his/her faithful service as our interim pastor during the past _____ [*number*] months. We rejoice in the work that he/she has done in this interim time. We thank him/her for leadership in our worship services and for sharing the Bible and its relevance to our daily lives. We are grateful for his/her pastoral care of those in special need, the sick and the sorrowing. Above all, we thank _____ [*name*] for helping us to prepare to welcome and to be ready to work with our new pastor, the Rev. _____.

Clerk:

_____ [*name*] has led the session, the deacons, and other leadership groups in this church in a review of our history and in a fresh examination of our tasks as together we enter a bright new chapter in the mission and ministry of _____ Church.

Personnel Chairperson:

_____ [*name*] has helped us to redefine our understanding of our part in the mission of Christ here and around the world. He/she has helped us to clarify our ministry to one another and guided us in our preparations for a new chapter in the life of _____ Church. His/her work among us allowed the pastor nominating committee to conduct its search for our new pastor with confidence and with a deliberate pace that enabled them to find that person whom we believe the Holy Spirit has chosen to lead us into the new era that lies before us.

Interim Pastor:

Friends and fellow Christians, it has been a privilege for me to serve you during the past _____ [*number*] months. While I regret giving up the relationships with this church, it is an important part of my task as your interim pastor to say good-bye and leave at the right time. [*Some additional personal words are appropriate here.*] It is not easy to say good-bye, but it is important. There can be no new beginning until there has been an ending, and today is the ending of my ministry in _____ Church. Therefore, I am returning to our clerk of session, _____ [*name*], my keys to this church building. Thank you,

_____ [*name*], and thanks to all the elders, deacons, and other church leaders and members for their guidance and support on the journey we have shared.

Clerk:

_____ [*name*], when you first received these keys on Sunday, _____ [*date*], you gave us your walking stick as a sign of the temporary interim nature of your ministry here. Since you asked that we return it to you when you were ready to leave, I do so now, with thanks and regret and with a prayer for God's warmest blessing on you and your ongoing ministry in other churches. May God walk beside you as you continue your journey to the kingdom's goal.

Interim Pastor:

Will the congregation please join me in the Litany for Concluding an Interim Pastorate found in the bulletin insert today.

A Litany for Concluding an Interim Pastorate

PASTOR: O God, you have bound us together for these _____ months as pastor and people in this beautiful place.

PEOPLE: **We have worked for the advancement of your kingdom, proclaiming the good news of Christ's mission.**

PASTOR: We give you thanks for the mutual ministry that we have shared in these days now past.

PEOPLE: **We thank you for your patience with us and for your never-failing presence.**

PASTOR: Now we pray, Be with us as we separate, that we may each continue our witness for Christ,

PEOPLE: **Living out the faith of the gospel in our lives in all the days ahead.**

PASTOR: May we always be close to each other in the glorious communion of saints, in this life and through eternity.

PEOPLE: **All this we ask for the sake of Jesus Christ, your Son, our Risen Redeemer and Victorious Savior. Amen.**

Interim Pastor:

Our closing hymn is "Rejoice, Ye Pure in Heart" [*or similar hymn*].

Annotated Bibliography

GENERAL RESOURCES

The Alban Institute
Suite 433 North, 4550 Montgomery Avenue, Bethesda, MD 28014-3341
Phone: 800-486-1318, ext. 244; 301-718-4407, ext. 244; fax for orders: 301-718-1966

> A multidenominational agency, the Alban Institute shares practical resources and ideas about congregations across denominational, hierarchical, and clergy–lay lines and works for congregations in four ways: research, publishing (many publications are listed in this bibliography), consulting, and training. Alban publishes a bimonthly journal, *Congregations*, and a quarterly newsletter, *Inside Information*. It offers memberships to individuals, congregations, governing bodies, and other institutions and gives significant discounts to all members on the purchase of its publications, programs, and services.

Association of Presbyterian Interim Ministry Specialists (APIMS)
c/o Office of Certification and Accreditation, Churchwide Partnerships, Room M003, 100 Witherspoon Street, Louisville, KY 40202-1396
AT&T phone: 0-700-462-7467 (0-700-GO APIMS).

> "APIMS is a not-for-profit organization dedicated to the furtherance of the religious and educational ends of the Presbyterian Church (U.S.A.) as they relate to Interim Ministry. APIMS exists to provide support for pastors, spouses, and families as well as

governing bodies within the Presbyterian Church (U.S.A.) who are involved with interim ministry and to provide information regarding placement, training, certification, and research in the specialized field of interim ministry" (APIMS Bylaws). APIMS publishes a quarterly newsletter, *The Bridge,* and an annual *Interim Pastor's Handbook* written by APIMS members to share interim ideas and experiences. APIMS meets as a part of the annual conference of the Interim Ministry Network (see entry below).

Churchwide Personnel Services, Call Referral System
Associate for Personnel Services, Churchwide Partnerships, Room M067, 100 Witherspoon Street, Louisville, KY 40202-1396
Phone: 502-569-5729

Personnel Services supplies blank personal information forms (PIFs) to interim pastors seeking placement and supplies PIFs of interim pastors to interim pastor search committees.

Presbyterian Distribution Services (PDS)
Room 2409, 100 Witherspoon Street, Louisville, KY 40202-1396
Phone: 800-524-2612 or 502-569-5000

PDS sells copies of the *Book of Confessions* and the *Book of Order,* Presbyterian Church (U.S.A.), and other denominational publications.

Interim Ministry Network (IMN)
916 Rolling Road, PO Box 21251, Baltimore, MD 21228-0751
Phone: 410-719-0777; fax 410-719-0795; CompuServe ID # 72712, 1765

An international ecumenical organization of interim pastors, interim consultants, and denominational leaders from more than twenty-five denominations, the network provides support, encouragement, training, and professional development for those involved in the leadership of congregations and other church organizations during interim periods. IMN offers an accreditation program for interim ministry specialists, sponsors an annual conference for professional development, worship, personal reflection, and mutual support, and publishes a bimonthly newsletter, *The In-Between Times.*

Presbyterian Interim Ministry Certification Board (PIMCB)
Office of Certification and Accreditation, Churchwide Partnerships, Room M003, 100 Witherspoon Street, Louisville, KY 40202-396
Phone: 502-569-5751

PIMCB supplies application packets and information about the certification process (see Appendix F).

CHURCH DEVELOPMENT
AND CHANGE

McCuen, R. Howard, Jr., ed. *The New Committee on Ministry Handbook*. Louisville, Ky.: National Ministries Division, Presbyterian Church (U.S.A.) 1994. Many issues and responsibilities facing committees on ministry (COM) are covered in this work. Contributors and editors include a number of moderators of COMs, presbytery executives, stated clerks, and General Assembly staff. Three sections focus directly on interim ministry and are of special interest to all presbytery executives and COM members. Several other chapters relate to aspects of interim work.

Mead, Loren B. *Critical Moment of Ministry: A Change of Pastors*. Bethesda, Md.: Alban Institute, 1986. This is a book for pastors and laypersons who lead congregations through changes in leadership. It tells how differently clergy and lay leaders experience such critical moments, what processes need attention, and what this means for the future of the congregation.

Mead, Loren B. *Changing Pastoral Leadership*. Washington, D.C.: Alban Institute, 1976. A guide for governing body executives, this book contains both theory and practical ideas for work with churches in transition (Out of Print).

Oswald, Roy M., and Speed B. Leas. *The Inviting Church: A Study of New Member Assimilation*. Bethesda, Md.: Alban Institute, 1987. Based on Alban Institute research, this book includes a self-study design for a congregation to use in assessing its assimilation process and includes many practical suggestions for keeping new members involved in church life.

Phillips, William J. *Pastoral Transitions: From Endings to New Beginnings*. Bethesda, Md.: Alban Institute, 1988. Phillips helps both clergy and lay leaders identify and address difficult experiences as they move through pastoral transitions.

Sawyer, David R. *Work of the Church: Getting the Job Done in Boards and Committees*. Valley Forge, Pa.: Judson Press, 1986. Suggestions for "directed servanthood" help a congregation move from faith to positive action; building an official board into a cohesive team gets the work done.

———. *The Process Tasks of the Interim Leader*. An article published in the *In-Between Times*, Newsletter of the Interim Ministry Network (address listed above), 1994, Vol. 14, Nos. 2, 3, 4. This article describes the special responsibilities of the interim pastor or other interim leader.

Schaller, Lyle E. *The Change Agent: The Strategy of Innovative Leadership.* Nashville: Abingdon Press, 1972. Schaller considers all aspects of the process of change—styles, tactics, power, conflict, and avoidance of polarization—and provides a knowledgeable approach to the dynamics of change.

————. *Survival Tactics in the Parish.* Nashville: Abingdon Press, 1977. Following a fictional pastor through nine years at a church illustrates concrete, proven tactics to restructure and restrengthen a parish.

Smith, Donald P. *Congregations Alive.* Philadelphia: Westminster Press, 1981. These practical suggestions help bring a church to life through partnership in ministry.

Toward Improvement in Ministry Series. *Pastoral Activities Index; Pastoral Performance Profile; Planning for Ministry; Guidelines for a Session Personnel Committee; Session Activities Index,* 1974, 1976, 1984. Although these books are dated, they are still helpful. Those in print are available from DMS (see earlier listing).

White, Edward A. *Saying Good-bye: A Time of Growth for Congregations and Pastors.* Bethesda, Md.: Alban Institute, 1990. A resource for meaningful and healthy partings, this includes examples of a farewell worship service and a litany for closure.

CLERGY SPIRITUALITY AND SELF-CARE

Hands, Donald R., and Wayne L. Fehr. *Spiritual Wholeness for Clergy: A New Psychology of Intimacy with God, Self, and Others.* Bethesda, Md.: Alban Institute, 1994. This book explains how to develop and maintain a psychologically healthy spirituality in relationship with others.

Oswald, Roy M. *Clergy Self-Care: Finding a Balance for Effective Ministry.* Bethesda, Md.: Alban Institute, 1991. Oswald focuses here on how to restore and maintain a balance in the physical, emotional, spiritual, and intellectual dimensions of life.

Pappas, Anthony G. *Pastoral Stress: Sources of Tension, Resources for Transformation.* Bethesda, Md.: Alban Institute, 1995. After exploring the creative possibilities for transformation inherent in clergy stress, this book offers help for renewal.

CLERGY TERMINATION

Oswald, Roy M. *Running Through the Thistles: Terminating a Ministerial Relationship with a Parish.* Bethesda, Md.: Alban Institute, 1978. Insight into termination styles and how they affect clergy and parishioners is enhanced by the use of real-life illustrations of special value to interim pastors, who face frequent terminations.

CONFLICT MANAGEMENT

Fisher, Roger, and Scott Brown. *Getting Together: Building Relationships as We Negotiate.* New York: Penguin Books, 1989. From the Harvard Negotiation Project, this book suggests ways to deal with difficulties as they arise. It takes the reader step-by-step through initiating, negotiating, and sustaining enduring relationships—in business, in government, between friends, and in the family—and gives insights useful to churches.

Halverstadt, Hugh F. *Managing Church Conflict.* Louisville, Ky.: Westminster/John Knox Press, 1991. Halverstadt describes an ethical process of conflict management and shows how respectfulness, assertiveness, accountability, and a focus on the larger common good can serve as Christian behavioral standards. Addressing church systems in conflict, he offers ways of constraining those who act as antagonists and of collaborating with those who act as opponents, based on twenty-five years' experience consulting in churches and coaching church leaders to manage church conflicts.

Leas, Speed B. *Discover Your Conflict Management Style.* Bethesda, Md.: Alban Institute, 1984. Here is an excellent tool for raising self-awareness, as well as valuable insights on the nature of conflict and its resolution. Leas describes six different strategies for managing conflict.

————. *Moving Your Church Through Conflict.* Bethesda, Md.: Alban Institute, 1985. A how-to loose-leaf manual for clergy and lay leaders, this book presents easily applicable concepts and practical strategies.

THE CONGREGATION AND SYSTEMS THEORY

Friedman, Edwin H. *Friedman's Fables.* New York: Guilford Press, 1990. Twenty-four strange and mischievous tales illuminate the paradoxical sides of the human dilemma. Some are a delight to read. Insightful and challenging, this book is useful in study groups, retreats, and counseling.

————. *Generation to Generation: Family Process in Church and Synagogue.* New York: Guilford Press, 1985. Using new and valuable insights from family systems theory, Friedman explores the emotional processes at work in three primary systems—congregational life, members' families, and the clergy's own family—and suggests possibilities for diminishing stress and increasing congregational health.

Parsons, George D., and Speed B. Leas. *Understanding Your Congregation as a System: The Manual.* Bethesda, Md.: Alban Institute,

1993. Using systems theory, the authors evaluate congregational life and readiness for change in seven key areas: strategy, process, pastoral and lay leadership, authority, relatedness, and learning. The Congregational Systems Inventory (CSI) is available separately from the Alban Institute.

Steinke, Peter L. *How Your Church Family Works: Understanding Congregations as Emotional Systems.* Bethesda, Md.: Alban Institute, 1993. Here is family systems theory applied to congregational life: psychologically sound, theologically grounded, and illustrated with practical case studies—one of the clearest, most direct statements of systems theory as applied to the church.

THE CONGREGATION'S DEVELOPMENTAL TASKS

Blazier, Kenneth D., ed. *Leader's Guide for a Local Church Workshop.* Valley Forge, Pa.: Ministers-at-Large Program, 1993. These five booklets are not sold separately: "Coming to Terms with History," Marcia Patten; "Discovering a New Identity," Hazel Ann Roper; "Shifts of Power," Jan Chartier; "Re-Thinking Denominational Linkage," Glenn H. Leach; "Commitments to New Leadership and a New Future," Floyd Welton. They may be ordered from Ministers-at-Large Program, American Baptist Church, Valley Forge, Pa., 19482-0851.

THE CONGREGATION'S SELF-STUDY

Blunk, Henry A. *Smaller Church Mission Study Guide.* Philadelphia: Geneva Press, 1978. This easily understood guide for conducting a church self-study is widely used in the denomination.

Carroll, Jackson W., Carl S. Dudley, and William McKinney, eds. *Handbook for Congregational Studies.* Nashville: Abingdon Press, 1988. The authors provide various techniques for analyzing congregational and community values, resources, strengths, weaknesses, and demographics and include ready-to-use survey forms.

INTERIM PASTORATES

Macy, Ralph. *The Interim Pastor.* Bethesda, Md.: Alban Institute, 1978. This theoretical and practical paper clarifies the unique contribution of the interim pastor.

Porcher, Philip G., Jr. *What You Can Expect from an Interim Pastor and an Interim Consultant.* Bethesda, Md.: Alban Institute, 1980. This guide tells lay leaders how to use fully the skills an interim pastor brings to the congregation in transition.

THE MULTIPLE STAFF CHURCH

Mitchell, Kenneth R. *Multiple Staff Ministries.* Philadelphia: Westminster Press, 1988. Mitchell outlines a method for studying the life of a ministering team and provides examples of successful group ministries, problems to be overcome, and ways to increase effectiveness and satisfaction. Particular attention is given to the role of the woman minister and to the increasing number of clergy couples.

Schaller, Lyle E. *The Multiple Staff and the Larger Church.* Nashville: Abingdon Press, 1980. This book helps members of multiple staffs to see their role and its context more clearly, with special emphasis on the roles of the senior minister and the associate minister and their relationship to each other and on the use of volunteers.

POWER, AUTHORITY, AND LEADERSHIP

Fletcher, John C. *Religious Authenticity in the Clergy.* Bethesda, Md.: Alban Institute, 1975. Fletcher explores three kinds of testing encountered by new pastors that are turning points of trust, credibility building, and authentication.

Harris, John C. *Stress, Power, and Ministry.* Bethesda, Md.: Alban Institute, 1978. This discussion of the issues of stress and power in clergy and laity's lives focuses on the personhood of clergy and their relationships with laypeople and church systems. A seven-session study guide is available for those who wish to study these issues in group settings.

Oswald, Roy M. *Power Analysis of a Congregation.* Bethesda, Md.: Alban Institute, 1988. This is a guide to analyzing personal and corporate power in a congregation.

TRANSITIONS

Bridges, William. *Managing Transitions: Making the Most of Change.* New York: Addison-Wesley Publishing Co., 1991. In a further development of the theme introduced in the earlier work listed below, Bridges suggests what can be done to keep the emotional impact of change from disrupting an entire organization and provides concrete guidelines for taking control of change.

————. *Transitions: Making Sense of Life's Changes.* New York: Addison-Wesley Publishing Co., 1980. Although not directly focused on church life, this book provides strategies for coping with difficult, painful, and confusing times in life and offers advice for negotiating endings, reorientation, and new beginnings.

VIDEO PACKAGE

Mead, Loren B., and William J. Phillips. *So Your Pastor's Leaving?* Bethesda, Md.: Alban Institute, 1988. This package combines a fifty-minute VHS videotape (with guide), which explains what to expect during the search process and allows opportunities for discussion by the search committee, with the Alban books *Critical Moment of Ministry* by Loren Mead and *Pastoral Transitions* by William J. Phillips.